THE SCIENTIFIC BASIS OF HINDUISM

VOLUME -1

ON PRANAVA MANTRA, TRI MURTHIS, MAHAVAKYAS, REBIRTH, THE SOUL AND ADVAITHA PHILOSOPHY

THE SCIENTIFIC BASIS OF HINDUISM

VOLUME -1

On Pranava Mantra, Tri Murthis, Mahavakyas, Rebirth, The Soul And Advaitha Philosophy

T Muralidharan

Notion Press

Old No. 38, New No. 6
McNichols Road, Chetpet
Chennai - 600 031

First Published by Notion Press 2016
Copyright © T Muralidharan 2016
All Rights Reserved.

ISBN 978-93-86009-81-4

INCARNATION

Incarnation forms the crux of Hindu Philosophy. The word is derived from the Latin root *caros* meaning flesh and is used to denote the appearance of a deity in flesh and blood or physical form. The concept of incarnation gives credence to the theory that the Trimurthis, Brahma, Vishnu and Maheswara are personifications of creation, sustenance and annihilation respectively, rather than being the Creator, Sustainer or Annihilator.

WHY BRAHMA HAS NO INCARNATIONS?

Brahma personifies creation. (Pro)creation, whether in plants or animals follows the same pattern. In humans, for example, sperms deposited in the vagina during coitus, move up the uterus, up the tube, finally reaching the fimbriated end of the Fallopian tube, which has a fanciful resemblance to a lotus. Here it meets with an ovum released from the ovary, and unites with it in a process called fertilization. This is the starting point of a new living being. In the case of plants, pollen, which represents the male sex cells, fall on the stigma of a flower (the stigma has the appearance of a lotus and is the terminal end of the female reproductive system), move down to the ovum and unites with it. Thus, whether it is a plant or animal, the terminal end of the reproductive system is the starting point of a new life, in other words Creation. Since there is no variation from this pattern whatsoever, no incarnation is assigned to Brahma.

WHY IS THERE NO INCARNATION FOR PARAMASIVA?

Paramasiva personifies Death. He depicts the various ways by which death is possible, namely, drowning, fire, strangulation, hanging, ingested and injected poison, animal attacks, death by weapons, etc. But, irrespective of the way in which death occurs, the proximate cause of death is only lack of oxygenation which is constant and hence no incarnation for Paramasiva either.

But with Vishnu, who personifies life in its many and varied ways, the matter is different. Life, whether in land, both land and water, as a mammal, human etc is each different and to represent each, a different physical form is ordained. This is the basis of incarnation.

Taking a panoramic view of the Hindu Philosophy, one cannot but marvel at the scientific knowledge the ancient Rishis possessed and how they mixed science with folklore to craft, what appears to be a story, but concealing between its lines, Science- pure science.

CONTENTS

ACKNOWLEDGEMENTS

I gratefully acknowledge the help and support of

- ✦ Swami Chidananda Swaraswathy who provided me with books and advice.
- ✦ Sri Ramakrishna Math, Purnattukara, Thrissur who provided me with books.
- ✦ Mr. Sudhir menon who helped me design the cover and the pictures.
- ✦ To my wife, Ratnarajalakshmy and family members Aparna, Avinesh, Aravind who shared with me sleepless hours in preparing the book
- ✦ Vimal who helped with photos
- ✦ Dr. Aparna nair who helped me with computer work.
- ✦ To Notion press for all that is behind this.

PREFACE

At the outset I question the propriety of my writing this book for two reasons: first, I know no Sanskrit and hence have not read any of the original Vedas, Puranas etc. which are written in Sanskrit, but relied on the translations and explanations of the verses given by experts in the field. (The Upanishads by Mridanandaswamy in Malayalam published by Sri Ramakrishna Math Trissur mostly). Secondly, I am an ordinary student of Science, without much exposure in the vast arena of scientific knowledge. Hence this is mostly a layman's attempt to understand some of the facets of the fascinating subject of Hinduism, meant for lay people, and hence mistakes and misinterpretations are bound to be legion.

Many learned people including Judges have, after careful assessment, noted that Hinduism is not a religion, but is a way of life. This is for various reasons: Hindus are not incarcerated in the ramparts of religious dogmas; there are no religious heads who overrule individual freedom. Hinduism does not denounce other religions and theist or atheist, believer or non believer, could all still be Hindus. A Christian calls a non believer in his faith as a heathen, a Muslim calls him a Kafir while a Hindu calls such a person a human. While there are umpteen numbers of Puranas, epics and other scriptures, a Hindu is not expected to know or follow any of these. Going to places of worship is not compulsory, nor worship itself. It demands nothing but contains everything. Moreover the pivot of Hinduism is the Vedas. Veda means knowledge. And knowledge means Science. When we see the Sun in the sky, we know it as a dazzling object, red or white in the sky. As our Scientific knowledge increases, we know the Sun as the pivotal point in the Solar System, with nine planets revolving around it; that, it is a mass of helium, is the source of all energy in the world and what not. And scientific knowledge changed the way of life from how our forefathers lived to how we live today. And that is why Hinduism guided by the Vedas is Science.

Vedas, like the Lord are not the creation of anyone. They, like the Lord, are supposed to have originated *de novo*. Veda Vyasa is credited with having passed on the Vedas to posterity through his disciples. Scriptures are the mainstay of any religion. The Holy Bible is the scripture of the Christians; the Holy Koran that of the Muslims, The Guru Granth Sahib that of the Sikhs and so on. Most religions have only one scripture. Probably conforming to the opinion that Hinduism is not a religion, consider the plight of a Hindu with:

Four Vedas and their Upavedas (subsidiary Vedas-numbering five).

The one thousand and eight Upanishads of which only one hundred and eight are known and twelve only recovered.

The one hundred and eight smruthis,

The six Darsanas.

The two epics (Ramayana, Mahabharata)

The eighteen Maha Puranas and another eighteen Upapuranas.

The Brahma Sutra and

The Bhagavad Gita

(The list is not complete.)

The Hindu scriptures are neither uniform in their content nor entirely divine in their concept. For example the Rig Veda, which extols Vishnu, Siva, Saraswathy and Indra, has, as its upaveda, Ayurveda which deals with an entirely different subject, namely the science of healing. The Yajur Veda details the ways yagnas are conducted and how Gods are worshipped but its Upa Veda is Dhanurveda which deals with how wars are fought, armoury, martial arts etc. The Sama Veda contains the same Mantras as in Rig Veda but tells us how these are chanted in a musical way, while yajnas are performed. Its Upaveda is Gandharva Veda which tells us about music and instrumental music. The Atharva Veda is at times considered not a Veda at all. It teaches us how to dodge dangers, protect from enemies, self defence, and the way to prosperity. It also deals with black magic. The Atharva Veda has two Upa Vedas namely Silpaveda which deals with construction and Artha Veda which deals with daily life, social structure, politics etc. Thus the Vedas teach us from mantras to music and construction to copulation- in short the stark realities of life.

For about six decades, I was an ordinary Hindu- which I still continue to be-going to the temple once in a while and praying many a God. I accepted the existence of God in whatever form they were pictured, never caring for the meaning of anything. But for more than a couple and a half decade, it had been nagging my mind that the scriptures of Hinduism had meanings more than what meet the eyes. My doubts were ratified when I once chanced on a lecture by the great scientist and scholar, Dr. N.Gopalakrishnan, and taking the cue from him, I began to think why whatever I was exposed to should not be analysed in a way different. And the result was marvellous. I found that whatever I had hitherto understood had a meaning, an explanation totally different and that Hinduism is nothing but science. If the question were to be raised as to why all the fanfare of Vedas Puranas etc, the answer is simple: it is understood better thus than as pure science. Of all the people studying science which run into trillions, what fraction retains any of what they had studied? Hardly any. But when presented as folk lore the retention is much better.

The Rishis who were the exponents of Hinduism were not ordinary people. They were people with intelligence beyond the extra ordinary genius and common sense beyond compare. It is preposterous to believe that they would conjure up the picture of a God wearing all sorts of weird articles as ornaments and dancing frantically when provoked. Or that another God should sleep over a snake in the middle of an ocean of milk as though there was no better place in the Universe. Or the Creator himself should stay in a lotus on the charity of Lord Vishnu, precariously balancing on His navel. If our scriptures abound in such descriptions, it only means one thing- that they are metaphorical and that the language of the scriptures is allegory.

If doubt still remains as to the allegoric nature of the Hindu scriptures, a couple of examples should suffice. It defies all sense of sensibility and symmetry to conjure up the figure of a person balancing ten heads. Yet Ravana is portrayed as one such and with good reason. In the yester years, war was fought amongst equals. If Sree Rama were to wage war with someone, the adversary should match Him in mettle and means; not otherwise. The ten heads and twenty hands of Ravana were meant to convey the message that Ravana had the wisdom of ten heads; that he knew the four Vedas and the six sastras and had the physical strength equivalent to ten persons. And being a king, he matched Sree Rama on all counts.

Our scriptures tell us that the god of love or Kamadeva has five flowers as arrows (called Sammohanastra) and any one shot with such arrows would send intense pangs of love on the viewer. The five flowers are: Asoka (saraca indica), Aravinda (lotus), Mandara, Mango and Neelolpala (vilvam as it is otherwise called). It is preposterous to believe that any one could string a bow and shoot arrows with such tender flowers which would be crushed by the mere handling, leave alone the archery. But if you stretch your imagination and understand that Kamadeva transformed the lady into one with the sweet fragrance and silky white texture of the Mandara flower, the crimson blush of the Asoka flower, the breasts like the unblown pink lotus buds, the ravishing smile of mango inflorescence and the languishing eyes like the vilvam flower, well even cold death (as personified in Sree Parameswara) was prompted to ejaculate !

When I started writing this book, I began to scribble whatever came to my mind, little realising what I was doing. Soon I realised that I was in the middle of an uncharted sea in a country boat and I was sailing nowhere. So I sat back and thought how I should go about writing. And I came up with the answer of dividing it into three or four volumes thus:

Volume I: The Pranava Mantra (AUM), The Trimurthis, etc.

Volume II: The Prasthana Thraya (Bhagavad Gita, Brahma Sutra and the Upanishads)

Volume III: The Epics Ramayana and Mahabharata

This I find convenient from many angles. I am old and do not know how far I could write. Secondly anybody reading and getting bored, could stop any time without the torture of going all the way to complete the book. Thirdly one need not pay for the uninteresting part of the book. Moreover this is my projection for the present and the format or contents may change any time.

1

Chapter

THE PRANAVA MANTRA

The syllable AUM (pronounced Uh-oo-m) contains the essence of Hindu Philosophy and is called the Pranava Mantra. It is formed of three incomplete syllables

A representing Vishnu, U representing Mahadeva and M representing Brahmadeva. How is the syllable AUM produced?

The air inside the body travels up from the navel and when it reaches the throat, the sound Uh (A in AUM) is produced. The air then travels up, touching the palate and cheeks and produces the oo (U in AUM) sound and when the lips close, the M sound is produced. Thus all parts from the throat up to the lip are involved in producing the sound AUM and hence AUM could be considered the basis of all letters and languages.

Explanation: A hollow pipe contains air but it produces no sound. Putting holes in it doesn't change the situation either. But forcing air through any one hole and partially closing the other holes results in melodious music, as in a flute. That means, sound is produced when resistance is offered to the passage of air under pressure. Our respiratory passages contain air but no sound is produced. When attempting to speak, or make a sound, the abdominal muscles contract, the diaphragm which separates the abdominal and chest cavities arches upward and squeezes air out of the lungs into the wind pipe and when the air reaches the throat, partial obstruction to the flow of air is offered by the opposing vocal cords and sound is produced.

When did the sound AUM first appear? "In the distant past, before the universe was created, before any life was possible, it was a vast expanse. And the first to appear was the Atma. The Atma heard the sound AUM resonating all over. And the Atma created the world."

Explanation: It may be difficult to understand this, but can easily be explained by an analogy. When a child is getting born, it produces no sound while coming out of the mother's womb. The body is practically lifeless and a few seconds elapse before the new born utters the first cry, drawing in air into the lungs and becoming viable. That means first the seemingly lifeless body representing the undifferentiated universe appeared and then the sound, synonymous with AUM. The sound AUM as it enters the body breathes life into the 'lifeless' body.

What is AUM? The Mandukya Upanishad begins with an elucidation of what AUM is. "All that we see are AUM. Its most lucid explanation is thus: Past, present or future, whatever existed, exist or will exist in the future are all AUM. Whatever has transgressed the three tenses is also AUM."

I sit in my room. There are myriad articles there. The doors, windows, chair, pencil, paper, torch, mirror or anything for that matter- all are AUM. There is a panel where once an A/C was fixed but now removed- that also is AUM. In future if I install an A/C that also would be AUM. And I imagine that in the far future I would convert my small house into a big shopping mall-that also would be AUM since anything that transgresses time- imagination is also AUM.

I step out. In the far distance I can see mountain stretches, trees, high rise buildings, slums, roads, factories etc. I look up: the azure sky, the multitudes of stars, the sun, moon, birds, airplanes-by definition, all are AUM. I take a spade and start digging. I have dug a pit. As I continue digging, water sprouts- I have created a well. The excavated soil has created a mound. I expand my digging and in the long run created a pond, and then a river and the soil dumped had successively created a hillock and finally a mountain. I have created a well, a pond, a lake, a river ad a mountain all with no extraneous material used, except perhaps a spade. Instead of a spade, I could as well have used any other implement and done the same thing. And in my stead, you or anybody else could have done the same thing. So what has a spade, me, you, any other implement, well, lake, river, mountain all have in common that makes all Brahmam? According to scientists, all these have two things in common, namely, all these occupy a certain space and all have a certain weight called its mass. Scientists call these as matter.

We have illustrated only a simple example. If instead of water, say, coal or gold or granite is struck by my digging over a prolonged period of time, does it change the position any way? Not at all. Upanishads still call them Brahmam and scientists still call them matter. In off shore drilling in the quest for oil, at times crude, at times natural gas is struck. Again, these are Brahmam to Upanishads and matter to science. In short, solid, liquid or gas, all are Brahmam or what scientists call, matter.

The Upanishads say that AUM and Brahmam are synonymous. If so, why then, should there be the two terminologies? Which means there is bound to be some difference, subtle though it be. We cannot see AUM. AUM is a sound we can hear but not see. And sound is a form of energy. So any form of energy we could feel but not see is also AUM. Like for instance electric, electro-magnetic, radiant, thermal etc. But Brahmam is matter which we can see. Thus AUM and Brahmam represent energy and matter respectively.

Matter, we have seen exists in the solid, liquid or gaseous states. How is it that these three equate? What is common to all these states? Water is a liquid at ordinary temperature but when heated, it evaporates and becomes water vapour which is in the gaseous state. The water vapour (steam) on cooling condenses and becomes water again. On extreme cooling, water becomes ice which is solid. Here matter has not changed, but something else changed which caused the same water to become a gas or a solid. This something is the molecular arrangement. That is, matter is composed of molecules and the way these are arranged determines whether water is in the solid, liquid or gaseous state.

Matter is not always mountain. The mountain may be broken down bit by bit and it successively becomes a boulder, a stone piece, a pebble, a grain and finally dust. And in all these states, it is still matter. The water in the ocean may evaporate and when completely evaporated, no water remains but water still exists in the evaporated state which can again condense and form water. You cut a pumpkin into two. You obtain two pieces of matter. Go on cutting and you get innumerable pieces of matter. And while cutting, you notice that you have cut the skin, the pulp, the seeds etc, all of which are matter by themselves. You cut an iron rod. You get two pieces of iron. Go on cutting. You get many pieces of iron. That is, matter may be composed of the same or different types of constituents. These constituents which make up matter are called elements.

Elements are basic chemical substances found in nature, not singly, but in combination with other elements to form mixtures and compounds. These elements, hundred and three in number, are arranged in a tabular form by scientists. This table is called the Periodic Table. The commonly spoken of elements are Hydrogen, Oxygen, Nitrogen, Carbon, Iron, Copper etc. Air is an example of a mixture of gases while water is a compound of hydrogen and oxygen.

What is the basis of arranging the elements in the periodic table? It is based on the number of atoms (protons in the atom, to be precise) in each element called the atomic number of the element. And atoms are the smallest part of an element which cannot be divided further (atom in Greek means indivisible). Atoms do not exist in the free state. The smallest part of an element which can exist in the free state is called a molecule.

An atom has a central core called the nucleus of the atom which is made up of positively charged particles called protons, and particles with no charge called neutrons. Usually all atoms have the same number of protons and neutrons. Negatively charged particles called electrons whirl around the nucleus in fixed orbits called shells. Usually the number of electrons equals the number of protons and hence atoms are generally electrically neutral. But sometimes an atom gains or loses an electron in chemical reactions or when colliding with other atoms. This results in a charged atom called an ion.

Atoms wield tremendous energy, when two atoms unite (called atomic fusion) or an atom splits (called atomic fission).This energy can annihilate the whole world or light up the whole world, as in atom bombs or nuclear reactors. (In Puranas, what is meant by Brahmastra with the ability to destroy the whole world may probably be this atomic bomb).

Sa ya eshonamai that atmam idam sarvam

That satyam sa atma That Tvm Asi Svetaketo iti.

(The infinitesimally minute aspect or core is the atma of the whole universe. That alone is the Truth, That is the Atma of all, O! Svetaketu That thou Art.). This quotation from the Chandogya Upanishad tells us what science teaches us about atom and its nucleus.

So now we have found that whatever exists, existed or is likely to appear in the distant future, whatever transgresses time, space and place, whatever is imagination, are matter and energy or in Upanishad parlance Brahmam and AUM. And, whether matter or energy, whether Brahmam or AUM, all have a positive charge, a negative charge and neutrality. And as implied in That Tvm Asi, the central core which is the atma of the entire universe is the nucleus of the atom- the creator, the peace maker, or the exterminator (Brahma, Vishnu, Maheswara).

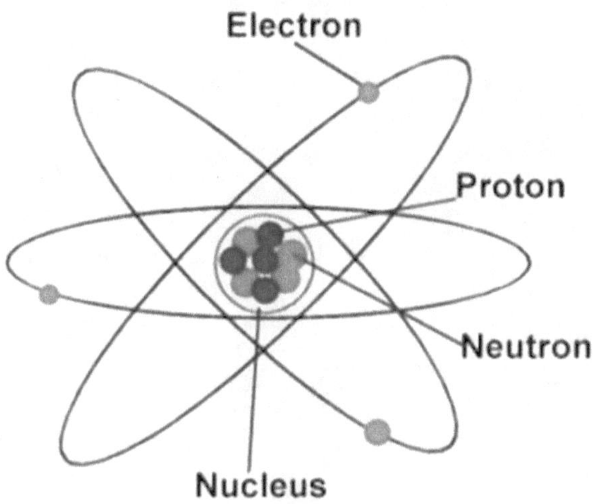

Structure of atom Atom of any element has a central nucleus, made of Protons and neutrons and an outer shell of electrons revolving around it in fixed orbits. The Protons are positively charged, Neutrons are electrically neutral and Electrons are negatively charged. Hence atoms are without charge.

2
Chapter

THE TRIMURTIS-BRAHMADEVA

The Principle AUM, as soon as it formed, split into its constituents, namely, A standing for Vishnu, U standing for Mahadeva and M standing for Brahmadeva, representing sustenance, annihilation and creation respectively. These three constitute the Trimurtis.

BRAHMADEVA

(Throughout this text the term Brahmadeva is used to denote Brahma of the Trimurtis so as not to confuse with the Brahmam which denotes the Para Brahmam)

Brahmadeva, the god of creation is portrayed as a God with four faces. He sits on top of a lotus flower, the long stalk of the lotus springing from the navel of Lord Vishnu. This precarious perch may seem at first sight rather quizzical, unless one realises that this is allegory at its probable best. The lotus springs from the navel of Lord Vishnu because, for one thing, Vishnu is concerned with sustenance and represents the nutrition of a growing foetus. Secondly, this posture of Brahmadeva is depicted only when Vishnu assumes the Ananthasayanam posture and not otherwise. The reason is that Vishnu in Ananthasayanam is in Palazhi or ocean of milk and ocean of milk is the sea littoral where pleasures abound and creation is the fruit of pleasure. He is the only God to possess white flowing beard and white hair, all others having escaped premature senility by consuming Amruthu (elixir) obtained by churning Palazhi (ocean of milk).The white hair and beard probably are meant to represent eternity and not premature senility. A youth can become old, an old man could become aged, an aged man can become wizened, and cannot ripen any further. He stays on, as long as his life is destined. And since Brahmadeva is not known to have evolved when, and stays on and on, He is portrayed as eternity.

Brahmadeva is the only God, for whom no temples are built, for whom no hymns are sung, to whom no offerings are made and whose worship is taboo. The story behind is that Brahmadeva and Lord Vishnu had a wager as to who would discover the frontiers of Parabrahma first. And up went Brahmadeva and down Lord Vishnu, with neither finding what they searched for. Beaten, Vishnu accepted defeat. But Brahmadeva, courting a pandanus flower for a witness, claimed to have seen the top of Parabrahmam. This invoked the wrath of Paramasiva, who cursed Brahmadeva that none would worship Him for a God, nor accept pandanus flower as offerings to Gods, being a false witness. Though the story is flowery, the fact may be that Brahmadeva personifies creation, and creation or rebirth is a concept a Hindu does not subscribe to-it is deliverance or Moksha (liberation from birth-death-rebirth cycle) that he wants. As for pandanus flower, anybody handling it is more than likely to bruise his hands for one thing and the flowers are unwieldy.

The only place and the only time Brahmadeva is worshipped is probably the Vaasthu Pooja performed when a house is newly constructed. Vaasthu pooja is for the presumptive deity, Vaasthu Purusha who is a human form lying spread on the entire plot where construction is aimed at. This is because a house is a creation, and when a creation is being undertaken, the creator is to be honoured.

The description of Brahmadeva raises many moot points. First, how could Brahmadeva, the size and weight of an adult, perch on a lotus hardly the size of his clenched fist? Secondly why should Brahmadeva be precariously perched on a lotus springing from the navel of Lord Vishnu? He could as well have chosen a much comfy place elsewhere. If it were mandatory that he should sit on a flower and flower only, why choose a lotus with a long stalk and hence much lesser stability than a short stalked silky and fragrant flower like rose?

The answer to all these questions is that the whole concept is metaphorical and not literal.

Let us examine what the role of Brahmadeva is. It is presumed to be creation. Creation is the process of bringing forth new ones. An artist creates a picture. A sculptor carves out a statue. Both do creative work. In the living world, plants and animals bring forth new ones by a process of reproduction. The difference between creation and reproduction is that creation is imaginative and non repetitive while reproduction is non imaginative and repetitive. Brahmadeva is concerned with both creation and reproduction. In plants reproduction may be by asexual or sexual methods while in animals reproduction is mostly by the sexual methods with stray instances of asexual reproduction. For sexual reproduction there are separate organs called reproductive organs. Strangely, the reproductive organs throughout the living world (plants and animals) are identical.

The reproductive organs in plants are clothed in flowers. Flowers are attractive, showy and usually odorous and contain both male and female reproductive organs. The male reproductive organs in plants are called stamen. Each stamen has a filament and a terminal anther. The anther contains pollen grains which fertilize the ovum situated in the ovary. The reproductive organs in the female are called the pistils. Each pistil has a stigma, style and an ovary which contains the ovum. Pollen grains liberated from the anther, fall on the stigma, travel down the style and fertilize the ovum.

It is strange that the sexual urge is present in plants as primitive as the alga Spirogyra and this plant manages its sexual urge even in the absence of any sex organ. In this plant, sexual reproduction occurs by a process called conjugation. Two filaments of this plant (these algae are filamentous) come side by side, kiss and fondle in their own primitive way and the protoplasmic material from one flows into the other, thus completing the conjugal process.

Human reproductive organs, both male and female (as representative of the entire animal world) bear a striking resemblance to their plant counterparts. The stamen resembles the penis, with the anther corresponding to the glans and the filament resembling the shaft of the penis.

The female reproductive organs in humans consist of two ovaries, the uterus, the Fallopian tubes and the vagina. The fimbrial end of the Fallopian tubes looks like the stigma of flower, the pistil looks like the Fallopian tubes and the ovary containing the ovule resembles the uterus with the fertilized ovum.

Reproduction (as a form of creation) takes place when during copulation, the sperms discharged into the vagina, move up the uterine cavity into the Fallopian tube meet with an ovum discharged from the ovary caught in the fimbria moves into the Fallopian tube, and their union results in the formation of a zygote or a baby in the making. The fertilized egg or zygote moves down the tube into the uterine cavity where it gets implanted and matures into the foetus.

A lotus full blown has the appearance of the fimbria. Brahmadeva sitting on top of the lotus has the same connotation as a fertilized human ovum at the fimbrial end or a pollen grain over the stigma of a flower. The long stalk of the lotus denotes the Fallopian tube in animals or the style in a flower. The nutrition for the developing foetus is derived from the mother (here Vishnu corresponds to the mother since He is concerned with sustenance.)

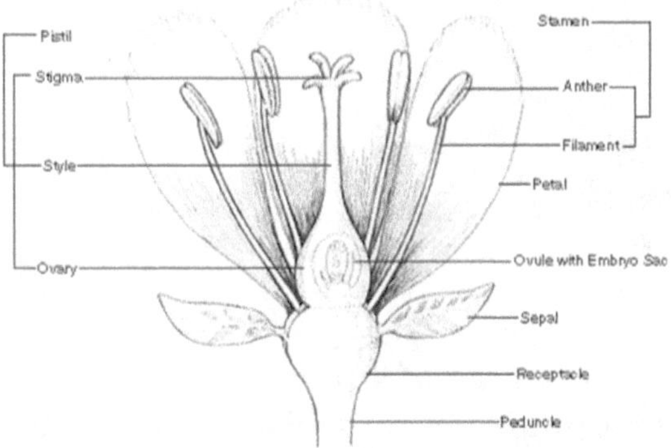

Section of a flower *The male reproductive organ is the stamen which consists of an anther and filament. The anther resembles the glans and the filament, the shaft of the human penis. The female reproductive organ or pistil consists of an ovary, style and stigma. The ovary with the ovule resembles the human uterus, the style, the Fallopian tube and the stigma, the fimbriae. The fimbria resembles lotus and ovum at the fimbria resembles Bhramadeva on top of lotus viewed upside down.*

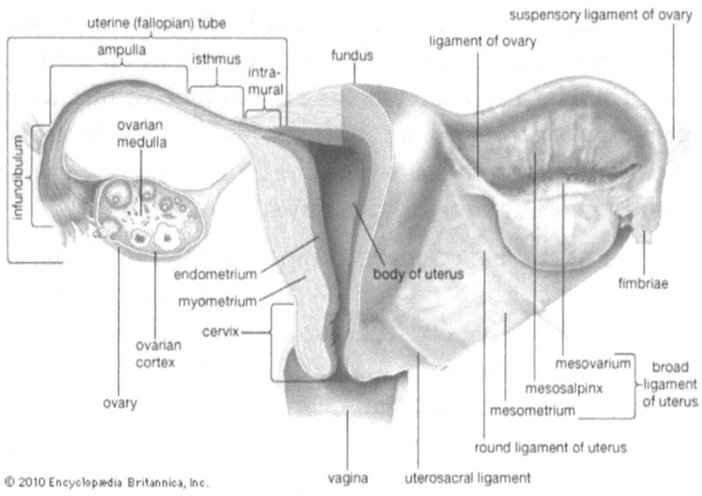

Brahmadeva on top of a lotus *Progressive reduction in size to demonstrate creation. Brahmadeva on top of the lotus resembles pollen grain on the stigma of a flower or ovum on the fimbrial end of the Fallopian tube (in the latter instance it looks like an inverted picture). Thus, whether in plants or animals, Brahmadeva portrays the process of procreation.*

3
Chapter

THE CREATIONS OF BRAHMADEVA

Sreemad Bhagavatham (One of the scriptures of Hinduism) details the creations of Brahmadeva thus:

The initial creations were: Thamas, Moham, Mahamoham, Thaamisram and Andha Thamisram.

Thamas is non recognition of one's self.

Moham is the feeling that "I am there in the body."

Mahamoham is the desire in sexual pleasures.

Thaamisram is the resultant ire when the desires are blighted.

Andha Thamisram is the feeling of dejection when the sensual pleasures are spoiled.

Brahmadeva was not happy with the sight of his creations. So he mentally paid obeisance to the Lord and with this pure mind started afresh his creative process, which resulted in the creation of his four 'Manasaputras' (sons born from thought or mind) namely Sanakan, Sanandan, Sanathanan and Sanalkumaran. They were confirmed celibates and when asked to take up creation, they were reluctant. The ire of Brahmadeva knew no bounds at the stance of his Manasaputras and his anger burst out from the middle of his eyebrows as a demigod. Brahmadeva called him Rudra and conferred eleven positions, eleven names and eleven wives to him. He implored Rudra to start creation. Rudra started creation in tune with his strength, character and form. Seeing the ferocious creations, Brahmadeva was horrified. He asked Rudra to stop creation of such figures, cleanse his mind by austerity measures and start creation afresh.

Further thought of creation gave Brahmadeva ten more Manasaputras. They were:

Mareechi	Krthu
Athri	Brigu
Angiras	Vasishtan
Pulasthan	Dakshan
Pulahan	Narada

They were called Prajapathis

From the lap of Brahmadeva originated Narada, from the big toe Daksha, from the prana (breath) Vasishta, from the skin Brigu, from the hand Krthu, from the navel Pulahan, from the ears Pulasthyan, from the face Angiras, from the eyes Athri, from the mind Mareechi, right breast Dhaman (who was a Prajapathi and his sons were Naran and Narayanan), from his back Adharma (and from it Mrithyudeva), from the heart Kama, from the brows anger, from the lips lobha (avarice), from the face the godess of speech, from the penis the seas, from the anus Niruthi representing sin, and from the shadow Kardhama Prajapathi. (The testicles are significantly not mentioned, thus alluding that he did not have any direct involvement in sexual reproduction.)

Thus the world originated from the mind and body parts, the shade and shadow of Brahmadeva.

But Brahmadeva fell prey to an evil instinct. His own creation Saraswathy had a great fascination for him. But his sons- Mareechi and others advised him to control his desires, since he was to set an example to the whole world. Bahmadeva was penitent at the words of his sons that he forsook his body which was taken up by the directions and became mist. Brahmadeva accepted, by assumption, another body.

Brahmadeva's thoughts on creation did not stop and from his thought the four Vedas evolved, one from each face: Rig Veda from the front face, Yajur Veda from the right face, Atharva Veda from the left face, Sama Veda from the face on the back.

The facets of Dharma-

> Daanam from the North face
>
> Daya from the West face.
>
> Tapas from the South face
>
> Sathyam from the East face

The Ashramas - Brahmacharyam (celibacy) from the east face

> Garhasthyam from the South face
>
> Vaanaprastham from the West face
>
> Sanyasam from the North face

The Upavedas - Ayur veda from the East face

> Dhanur Veda from the South face
>
> Gandharva Veda from the West face
>
> Sthapathyam or silpa Veda from the North face

The Epics (the Itihasa) which form the fifth veda were created from the four faces.

Adyatma Sastra, Vaidika Sastra, Agriculture, Business, Politics and the Gayathri Mantra all evolved from the faces of Brahmadeva.

From the heart - AUM

From the hairs - Usnik (a prosody with 28 letters)

From the skin - Gayathri (a prosody with 24 letters)

From the flesh - Thrishnup (a prosody with 44 letters)

From the veins - Anushtup (a prosody with 32 letters)

From the bones - Jagathy (a prosody with 48 letters)

From the marrow - Pangthy (a prosody with 40 letters)

From the breath - Brihathy (a prosody with 36 letters)

From the Prana - Ka to Ma (25 letters-Vargakshara)

From the body - Aa to Ou (16 Swaras)

Sense organs - Sha, Sa, ha.

From the strength - Ya, Ra, la, Va.

From the amorous exploits - The seven Swaras of Music (shadjam, Rishabham, Gandharam, Madhyamam, Panchamam, Daivatham and Nishadam)

After assuming another form, Brahmadeva began to ponder over creation. Though the Prajapatis who were entrusted with creation were doing their work, the process of creation was not making pace. Brahmadeva sought the reason for this and on this thought His body split into two. The bodies thus separated were called Kayam and from these two evolved, one a man and the other a woman. The male was swyambhoo Manu and the female became his consort Satarupa. And the whole human race came to be as a result of man-woman intercourse. Manu and Satarupa had five children, two males namely Uttanapadan and Priyavrathan and three daughters- Aakriti, Devahooti and Prasooti. Aakriti was married to Ruchi Prajapati, Devahooti to Kardhama Prajapati and Prasooti to Daksha Prajapati and their progeny filled the world.

4
Chapter

ANALYSIS OF CREATION

Creation is the process of making a new object and may refer to a living or an inanimate object, or for that matter anything in the Universe. Reproduction on the other hand, is the process of creating the replica of something. Brahmadeva represents both creation and reproduction, whether in imagination, as matter in its many and varied forms or as energy in its diverse modalities, or as life in part or in its entirety, or a semblance of it as in a shadow.

Brahmadeva did not create objects the way a potter at the wheel moulds a pot or a smith beats metal to produce ornaments, utensils or cutlery. In fact, nowhere is it mentioned that Brahmadeva created anything. Let us take an overview of what Brahmadeva did.

The initial creations of Brahmadeva were Thamas, Moham, Mahamoham, Thamisram and Andha Thamisram. They originated in His thoughts and hence were not material. On the other hand, they were only imaginations or passions or emotions. The first stage of copulation in animals (or for that matter plants) is the instinct or urge to copulate. The five initial creations alluded to Brahmadeva refer to this urge. The pangs of love from the first stage of sight to the terminal stages of madness and death are beautifully personified in the reference to the initial creations of Brahmadeva. Bharatha Muni in his famous Natya Sastra which details the pre requisites for the Theatre, explains the ten stages through which a lover passes through, thus: "Mana,Sangama, Sankalpa, Jagratha, Krisatha, Aarathi, Hreethyaga, unmada, Mohalasya, Anthya: evam ankada dasa dasa." Mana is the desire to unite, sankalpa is the flowery imagination, Jagratha is the state of sleeplessness; Krisatha is becoming lean; aarathi is aversion to food; hreeethyaga is shamelessness; unmada is madness, mohalasya is unconsciousness and anthya is death. Evam ankada dasa dasa means these are the ten stages of Kamadeva (God of love). Evidently, madness and death are not compatible with creation or procreation and this is the reason why it has been said that Brahmadeva was not satisfied with the last of his creations.

The next in line of creations was the four Manasaputras of Brahmadeva namely Sanakan, Sanandan, Sanathanan and Sanalkumaran. They were said to be confirmed celibates and refused to take up creation when asked to do so by Brahmadeva. This probably alludes to the pre-pubertal stage when a child is celibate and incapable of creation. These creations were not physical but imaginations of Brahmadeva's mind, and is the reason why they were named Manasaputras. That is, imaginations of whoever is the creator.

After the first set of four Manasaputras, the second set of ten Manasaputras was the next in line of Brahmadeva's creations and they were called Prajapathis. They were capable of creation. The term Prajapathi in Sanskrit has meanings like penis, king, Vishnu, Brahmadeva etc. Obviously here the term signifies the fully erect penis, poised to strike, brimming with semen and capable of creation when directed to the correct milieu.

From the lap of Brahmadeva originated Narada, from the big toe, Daksha, from the prana (breath) vasishta, from the skin Brigu, from the hand Krthu, from the navel Pulahan, from the ears Pulasthyan, from the face Angiras, from the eyes Athri, from the mind Marichi, right breast Dhaman, from the back Adharma, from the heart Kama, from the brows anger, from the lips lobha (avarice), from the face the goddess of speech, from the penis the seas, from the anus Niruthi representing sin and from the shadow Kardhama Prajapathi. All mentioned in this list help in creation and hence are part of the creative process. They probably represent what psychologists call extra genital erotic points which have a great role in foreplay before erection and ejaculation or the creative process. Alternatively, it could also represent vegetative (asexual) reproduction in plants and some animals like Amoeba and hydra. It is said that Brahmadeva fell prey to an evil instinct and that was His attraction to Saraswathy, His own creation and hence His daughter equivalent. This probably represents self pollination and is regarded as not a healthy method of reproduction.

SYNOPSIS OF CREATION OF HUMANS

1. First step in creation is the desire to copulate. This is the sexual urge and is evident in plants and animals. This sexual urge may progress to the level of madness and death. This is cited as the first creations of Brahmadeva – Thamas, moham, mahamoham, thamisram and andha Thamisram.

2. The second stage of creation is the creation of the Manasaputras. The first set of four manasaputras denotes mental copulation. The still celibate stage where erection and ejaculation has not started is probably what is referred to here. (Probably the 8-11 years of age or the pre pubertal age.). There is a fancy, a curiosity to know about the opposite sex.

3. The third creation of Brahmadeva is rudra,a horrifying figure,over the creation of which Brahmadeva was unhappy. This probably alludes to masturbation where still no creation take place.

4. The second set of manasaputras, ten in number, result in the production of Prajapatis. Prajapatis are those capable of creation. Obviously this refers to erection followed by ejaculation which can result in reproduction. This probably refers to the pubertal stage- age twelve upward.

5. The fifth creation of Brahmadeva is from the different parts of His body and Atma. Obviously this denotes vegetative reproduction in plants and some animals where offspring develop from different parts of the parent body- new plants arise from the stem, leaves, seeds, roots etc of plants and new organisms develop like by binary fission in amoeba or budding in Hydra.

6. The sixth creation of Brahmadeva is the grand finale-setting the stage ready for human beings to evolve. Take a look at how this is achieved:

    a. Creation of the Vedas- Veda means knowledge. The Vedas cover a vast array of human endeavour- practically everything.

b.   Creation of the Dharmas.

c.   Creation of the four Ashramas: Brahmacharyam (the celibate stage) Grihasthasramam (married and living with family) Vanaprastham (retired life as though living in a forest) and Sanyasam (detached and living as an ascetic).

d.   Creation of the Upavedas (Ayurveda, Dharma Veda, Silpa Veda and Gandharva Veda.

e.   The Yajnas.

f.   The stages of Brahmacharya.

g.   The various metres in Poetry.(Gayathri, Anushtup, Thrishtup, Jagathy, Pangthy, Brihathy etc.

h.   The letters of the alphabet.

i.   Music.

Finally, having set the world as a nursery for humanity to develop, man as a sexually and only sexually propagated animal developed. For this to happen, Brahmadeva after assuming another form, split into two and from one part a male and from the other part a female evolved. The male was Swayambhoo Manu and the female, Satarupa. And the whole mankind evolved from man-woman intercourse.

Creation of other animals is explained thus in the Brihadaranyaka Upanishad: Satarupa was ashamed that Manu who was her father equivalent should have seduced her. So she tried to vanish and assumed the form of a cow. But Manu, knowing her designs became a bull and mounted her, thus ensuring the creation of the progeny of cows. Satarupa became a mare and Manu a stallion and thus evolved the horses. Satarupa became a she ass and Manu an Ass and thus the lineage of asses came to be. He became a goat when she tried to masquerade in a she goat and thus the genealogy of goats was established. And the process of creation of all animals happened because of the intercourse between Manu and Satarupa in their varied forms as animals.

Leaving aside Brahmadeva and His creations, let us for a moment come to practical life. Biologically, in humans, when did creation start? It is pertinent to note that while Brahmadeva is credited with creation, living organisms are endowed with the power of procreation, meaning their creation is production of young ones. When childhood gives way to adolescence, when a boy turns into a youth, he notices many things: hairs appear above his lip, in the armpit, and in the groin, voice deepens, and folks of the opposite sex whom he hitherto detested offer a pleasant affinity. His gaze shifts to curves and he notices a hardening in the groin which has to be released somehow. He mentally copulates resulting in a blighted creation. And real creation starts only with man-woman intercourse.

And that precisely is what hitherto has been said of the creation of Brahmadeva. The initial creations refer to the laying of the foundation for creation like the desire to copulate. The manasaputras refer to the mental copulation which is all imaginary and unreal creations. And before man is created, all that he needs when born, like knowledge (Vedas), medical and other skills (Ayur Veda, Gandharva Veda, Silpa Veda, Artha Veda), the code of conduct, the stages through which man passes (the four Asramas-Brahmacharyam, grihasthasramam, Vanaprastham and sanyasam), language, rhyme and prosody, and music await his arrival. And then, only then is man created (not by Him, of course)!

And so what did Brahmadeva create? He did not create human beings, or any of the millions and millions of organisms in the Universe. His consort is Saraswathy but no child is born of Him to Her. He set the stage ready so that life propagates by itself. In other words, He is not the creator but personifies creation. Skin or shin, hair or air, ire or mire, shade or shadow- anything about Him means creation.

5
Chapter

THE TRIMURTIS-MAHAVISHNU

MAHA VISHNU

Maha Vishnu is the first of the Trimurtis and represents the syllable A in AUM. (This may seem unacceptable, as creation should precede sustenance and hence Brahmadeva should be the first. This is explained in the scriptures thus: Though the Principle AUM split into three, of all the Principles, A is dominant, being all pervasive and universal. Hence He is reckoned as the first among the Trimurtis). His abode is described as Palazhi (literally meaning ocean of milk), where he reposes in a reclining posture in the bed formed of the coils of the serpent king, Anantha with the thousand hoods of Anantha forming a canopy over the reclining Lord. His feet are borne by Goddess Lakshmi and his four hands hold, the conch, the chakra or wheel, the maze and lotus flower. From the navel of the Lord emanates a full blown lotus borne on its long stalk atop which Brahmadeva engages in His work of creation.

The description of Lord Vishnu, like all or many others in the scriptures is an example of allegory at its best. Walking along a sea shore and gazing at the sea, the racing waves buffeting against the shore and smashing into smithereens imparts a milky colour to the sea. This is Palazhi or ocean of milk. The world as a turbulent mess is alluded here. Amid the worldly turbulence and pleasures- for pleasures abound near the sea littoral and not in mid ocean- the Lord reposes unperturbed. Psychologists have long held that snake is symbolic of sex, a finding which our Sages said ages before. The fact that the Lord had enslaved, not just any ordinary snake, but the king of all snakes symbolises his conquest of worldly pleasures at their very summit. Goddess Lakshmi at His feet speaks of His command over worldly wealth and treasures.

It is significant that the serpent bed- Ananthasayanam-posture of the Lord is only in Palazhi and the lotus springing from the navel of Lord Vishnu is only in relation to the Ananthasayanam posture. This is because, pleasures and creation go hand in hand and hence the apt place for these is the littoral region of the sea or sea shore as mentioned above.

A colourful anecdote speaks of the conquest of Lord Vishnu over sensual pleasures. Indra, chieftain of the Devas (Gods), fearing that the Lord in penance would rob him of his position, sent the celestial danseuse, Ramba to disrupt the penance of the Lord. Vishnu, sensing Indra's designs, created a far exquisite beauty and presented her to Indra. Since she was born from the thigh of the Lord, she came to be known as Urvasi (meaning born from the thigh).

The hands of the Lord are descriptive. Of the four, one holds a conch. The conch is the symbol of war. Blowing the Conch was the harbinger of war in older times and is akin to sounding the bugle in present day warfare. The conch in His hand denotes that He is a marshal of war. The wheel in His second hand signifies the wheel of time. It denotes that He has absolute command of time. Any one slain with the wheel was never reborn, thus liberating him from the birth-death-rebirth cycle. Maze is a weapon of straight fight, of close combat. It indicates righteousness and earnestness. An arrow could be sent at an enemy unseen, not a maze. The lotus denotes the heart- the soft heart always accessible to devotees. Sreevalsam is the black mole on the Lord's bosom. The story is that the Sage Brigu in a fit of anger stamped his foot on the Lord's bosom which He retained as a black mole ever afterwards. This speaks of the extreme humility and tolerance on the part of the Master of the Universe.

The complexion of the Lord is variously described. He is often spoken of as Shyamavarnan, Karvarnan, Mukilvarnan etc meaning black complexioned or one with the colour of the clouds. On the other hand, at many places, He is described as azure coloured. The two may seem contradictory unless one remembers that the descriptions are always allegoric. Azure colour denotes vastness, like, for example, the azure sky, the deep blue ocean or the mountain ranges. The black colour, on the other hand, portrays truthfulness. Black has no shades or hues and whatever colour mixes with black, only black remains. Seven colours in a disc produce white when rotated, but black rotated with whatever colour, only black remains.

The robe of the Lord is yellow. Yellow colour stands for serenity.

6
Chapter

THE INCARNATIONS OF VISHNU

Among the Trimurthis, or for that matter amongst all the Gods, only with reference to Vishnu is the term incarnation applied. Incarnation or Avtar is the assumption by the Lord of a form, to achieve a goal. Mahadeva had assumed the role of a hunter, that of a nomadic basket maker and so on, but these do not qualify to be called incarnations.

The incarnations of Lord Vishnu are ten in number and these are called the Dasavatharam. These are:

a. Matsya (fish)

b. Koorma (tortoise)

c. Varaha (wild boar)

d. Narasimha (Hind of man-Torso of Lion)

e. Vamana (Brahmin Boy)

f. Parasurama

g. Sree Rama

h. Balarama

i. Sree Krishna

j. Kalki

MATSYA AVATAR

Incarnation of Lord Vishnu as fish was to retrieve the Vedas the Asura Hayagreevan stole from the face of Brahmadeva.

King Satyavrata was an ardent devotee of Lord Vishnu. One day, as he was offering libation to spirits of ancestors in the river, a small fry appeared in the consecrated water he held in his hollowed palm. He transferred the fish to a small vessel, but the fry began to rapidly increase in size and soon became too large to be held in the vessel. So the king transferred it to a small pond and from there successively to a lake, a river and finally to the sea as the fish, rapidly growing in size, outgrew all its containers. Once in the sea, to the astonishment of Satyavrata, the fish began to speak: "You have cared for me and protected me all these while and now you are deserting me with none to protect me." The king realised that the fish was none other than Vishnu. "On the seventh day hence, the great deluge would engulf the whole Universe. You have to collect seeds of all plants and keep them in your hand. Go on meditating on me and when you are caught in the deluge and rattling, a boat would appear carrying the Saptharshis (the seven Rishis or sages.) You have to board the boat and when you see me in this form, fasten the boat to my mast, all the time meditating on me. You will be carried safely and at the end of the deluge, on the seventh day the Asura Hayagreeva would be slain and the stolen Vedas restored to Brahmadeva. So saying the fish disappeared only to reappear and enact whatever was said. And with the Vedas returned to His face, Brahmadeva began to continue his work of creation.

KOORMA AVATAR

Incarnation of Lord Vishnu as Tortoise: Once, Sage Durvasa received a divine garland of captivating smell and exquisite looks. Considering him, an ascetic, as unfit to don such a precious garland and deliberating on who would be the most apt candidate to be presented with the garland, he finally chose Indra as the nominee for the precious piece. Cautioning him to use the garland carefully without causing damage to it, Sage Durvasa presented the garland to Indra. As a prelude to using the garland, Indra kept it on the elephant's head, while parting his hair. The intoxicating smell of the flowers of the garland attracted a swarm of bees which covered the elephant's head and face. The frenzied bull tore apart the garland and trampled over it, much to the horror of Indra. The irate Durvasa cursed Indra that he and his coterie all became uncouth and aging. Indra was aggrieved and begged Durvasa for redemption from the curse. Durvasa, mollified, advised him to consume the elixir obtained by churning Palazhi. Indra sought the help of Brahmadeva in resolving the riddle of churning Palazhi. Brahmadeva pleading inability guided him to Paramasiva and all three went to Lord Vishnu.

Maha Vishnu dictated the instruments for churning Palazhi. Since the Devas would not be able to accomplish the task by themselves, the help of the Asuras had to be sought. The churning rod was to be the mountain Mandhara, the cord, the snake king Vasuki. Asuras on the head end and Devas on the tail end of Vasuki churned and as the churning progressed, suddenly the grip on one side slipped and the mountain began to sink into the ocean. All assembled panicked and implored Vasudeva to come to their rescue. And Lord Vishnu, assuming the form of a huge tortoise lifted the sinking mountain and when it began to rise high sat on the mountain top preventing it from rising further.

The gruelling experience was too much for Vasuki and it began to vomit. Vishnu, knowing that the whole Universe would be burnt in the venom of Vasuki known as Kalakootam, sought the help of Mahadeva. In an instant, Paramasiva gulped the deadly venom. Sree Parvathy realising that Paramasiva would be burnt by the deadly venom, instinctively choked His throat, preventing it from descending any further. Fearing that the venom might be spat out by Paramasiva, thus annihilating the whole world, Vishnu choked His throat from above. Thus the venom became incarcerated in the throat of Paramasiva, earning Him the name Neelakanda or the one with blue neck.

The churning now began to yield results. Kamadhenu, Airavatham (the white elephant) and a host of other articles surfaced and finally the elixir. No sooner did it appear than the Asuras disappeared with it, much to the chagrin and dismay of the Devas. Vishnu promised to retrieve the lost elixir. And assuming the form of Mohini, the most tantalizing feminine form ever, He retrieved the elixir to the Devas.

VARAHA AVATAR

Incarnation of the Lord as a wild boar:

Four sages- Sanakan, Sanandan, Sanathanan and Sanalkumaran went to pay obeisance to MahaVishnu but were intercepted by the sentries Jayan and Vijayan. The irate sages cursed them to be born as Asuras for three successive births until Lord Vishnu slew them and granted them salvation. Thus they were born to Sage Kasyapa and his consort Diti as Hiranyakshan and Hiranyakasipu.

Hiranyakshan and Hiranyakasipu wielded considerable power on the strength of a boon granted by Brahmadeva.

Haughty and invincible, Hiranyakshan wanted a suitable enemy and finding none chose the sea for an enemy and brandishing a maze began battering the waves. Horrified, Varuna, Lord of the seas went to Vishnu for help. Vishnu, fuming, assumed the form of a wild boar jumped out of the nostril of Brahmadeva. The Asura, snatching the Earth hid in the nether world. And that invited his end at the hands of Lord Vishnu who retrieved the Earth and kept it in its place.

NARASIMHA AVATAR

Incarnation of Lord Vishnu as Narasimha- torso of lion and hind of man:

Hiranyakasipu, knowing the fate of Hiranyakshan felt that his strength would not guard him from certain death, began to acquire new arsenals. With this view, he began to do penance and appeased Brahmadeva, who conferred on him the boon that no being in animal or human form, at no time of the day or night or no weapons could kill him; nor would he be slain on earth, sky or the nether world. Having thus secured what seemed to be a fool proof boon, he began tormenting people, conquered Indra and mauled ascetics. He conquered all three worlds. He forbid chanting Mantras in praise of Brahma, Vishnu or Maheswara and wanted everyone chant his name and sing hymns in praise of him. But his son Prahlada would have none of this. He had an innate devotion to Lord Vishnu, chanting His names and singing hymns in praise of Him. This enraged Hiranyakasipu and he warned the lad many a time and tormented him in many ways. One day, enraged at his son's insolence, Hiranyakasipu challenged his son to show the deity he worshipped. Prahlada said he was omnipresent and his father smashed a pillar with his maze on being told that the God he worshipped was there in the pillar as well. And indeed from the battered pillar emerged Lord Maha Vishnu in the form of Narasimha-half lion and half man and lifting Hiranyakasipu off the ground plunged the lion claws into his chest keeping him on the Lord's knees, thus fulfilling all the requirements needed for his death.

VAMANA AVATAR

Incarnation of Lord Vishnu as a celibate Brahmin boy:

Vamana was born as the son of Adithi and Kasyapa Prajapathi in fulfilment of a boon granted by Maha Vishnu to Adithi who wanted the Lord as her son to conquer Mahabali and return the Indra title to her son vanquished by Bali. Mahabali was a great philanthropic king who ruled his land to the praise of his subjects. He never used to turn away anyone empty handed whenever his assistance was sought. Vishnu thought it fit to capitalise on this trait. He assumed the form of a celibate dwarf Brahmin boy and asked for three feet space of land to do penance. Sukracharya, the teacher of the Asuras, knowing that the boy was none other than Vishnu, tried to prevent Bali from granting the wish, but Bali would not turn down the wish of anybody, least of all, that of a Brahmin boy. So Vamana measured- with the first foot he measured the whole world and the nether world, with the second, the Heavens and with the third at Bali's request, on his head, pushing him to the nether world.

PARASURAMA

The Lord incarnated as Parasurama to alleviate the sufferings of Mother Earth, who bore the weight of wicked men.

Parasurama was born as the fifth son of sage Jamadagni and Renuka. His life was marred by a series of killings. He killed his mother and siblings when asked to do so by his father, but prayed for their return when asked by the delighted father what boon he wanted. He killed Karthaveerarjuna, when the king had his father's sacred cow stolen. And when the slain king's sons retaliated by killing his father Parasurama killed them and the entire race of Kshathriyas. To atone his killings, he gifted all the land he had to sage Kasyapa and went to the Mahendra mountain for penance

Parasurama is credited with the creation of the land Kerala when he flung his divine axe from Gokern, reclaiming the land till Kanyakumari.

Parasurama was Guru to Karna whom he taught martial arts, but when he knew that Karna was actually a kshathriya in disguise as a Brahmin, he cursed Karna that whatever he had learnt would not stand him in good stead at times of need.

SREERAMA

Incarnation of Lord Vishnu as the perfect man.

The Avtar of Lord Vishnu as Sree Rama marks perfectionism in human sculpting. Sree Rama was the embodiment of human virtues, repository of human values and receptacle of feminine passion. Born of the Yaga fire as the eldest son of King Dasaratha, Sree Rama was nominated heir to the throne by King Dasaratha, but to fulfil the boon given by his father to his step mother, he willingly forsook the sceptre and spent the prime years of his life in the wild. Here he loses his wife and in her pursuit kills a whole army of Rakshasas, thus fulfilling his life mission of relieving the Earth of wicked elements.

BALARAMA

The eighth incarnation of Lord Vishnu:

Balarama was born as the seventh child of Vasudeva and Devaky. At the time of their marriage,a divine averment proclaimed that Devaky's eighth child would be the assassin of Kamsa. Enraged, Kamsa kept Vasudeva and Devaky in captivity for fear of life. As each child was born, Kamsa meticulously banged its head against a rock assuring its certain death. But when Devaky conceived the seventh time, Lord Vishnu transferred it to the womb of Rohini, another wife of Vasudeva. Thus Balarama was born to Rohini, who became his surrogate mother. Balarama is supposed to be the human form of the serpent king Anandan or Adi Seshan. He accompanied Krishna in all his pursuits. He had the plough as his weapon.

During the Kurukshetra war, when Krishna became Arjuna's charioteer, Balarama went on pilgrimage. His death is curious. The Yadava tribe after the Kurukshethra war lasted only for thirty six years. During the last days of His life Balarama went on penance under a tree. At this time a white snake crawled through his mouth and descended down, carrying His soul down through the sea to the nether world (pathalam).

SREE KRISHNA

The incarnation as Sree Krishna is the ninth of the Lord. With the professed aim of annihilating the wicked, Sree Krishna was born to Vasudeva and Devaky in captivity. When born, He had His fully divine form and implored Vasudeva to exchange Him for the baby born to Nandagopan and Yesoda at Gokulam. The whole kingdom of Mathura was lulled into a deep slumber, the shackles unbound, the prison gates opened, all by divine will and Vasudeva marched past the snoring guards with the babe Krishna. The drizzling did not deter Vasudeva, for the thousand hoods of Aadi Seshan formed a canopy over the basket and the babe, the river Yamuna parted for Vasudeva with the divine child to advance. At Gokulam, without any body being aware, Vasudeva exchanged Sree Krishna for the baby Yoga Maya (Yoga Maya is the supreme divine feminine power) born to Yesoda. As soon as Vasudeva returned to Mathura, the prison gates closed, the shackles closed in on Vasudeva and the changeling began to cry. The woken up guards brought the tidings of the baby's arrival to Kamsa who hastened to the prison. Seeing the baby a female, none the less taking no chances, Kamsa, holding the baby's ankles, swirled the child for banging against rock, but the babe slipped off the giant's hands into the thin air. There, in all Her divine radiance, Yoga Maya mocked Kamsa that valour should not be directed at women and children. His assassin is born in the world and the sooner he found out, the better for him. Panicked, Kamsa began trying every means of eliminating the child, in the bargain losing many of his accomplices like Poothana, Sakatasuran and others.

Sree Krishna grew up in Gokulam as the cynosure of young and old, male and female alike. With His famed flute, He stole the hearts of cows and their herds. He gave moksha to the two sons of Kubera, who were penalised into becoming trees at the curse of Narada, He showed to Yesoda that he is the master of the Universe by showing the entire Universe in His mouth, when His mother chided

Him for swallowing mud. When an irate Indra inundated Gokulam, lashing it with thunder and lightning, Sree Krishna, heeding to the call of the residents, spun the Govardhana Mountain on His finger as an umbrella, thus protecting them from the wrath of Indra. Sree Krishna was a true comrade to his friends and a lover to every Gopika, with whom He performed the famous Rasalila, giving to each the impression that He was solely with her. Thus He reciprocated to their chaste devotion. He married Rukmini and in addition had seven wives namely Sathyabhama, Kalindi,Jambhavathy, Mithravinda, Sathya, Bhadra and Lakshmana and when He liberated the sixteen thousand virgins incarcerated in Narakasura's court and assumed their guardianship, the tally rose to sixteen thousand and eight. SreeKrishna chastised Kalindi of its polluted waters by driving away Kaliyan, whom He battered by His dance on the serpent hood, to the Ramanaka island whence the serpent came.

Sree Krishna became the exponent of peace when mediating for the Pandavas and the marshal of war when peace efforts failed to coerce Duryodhana to part with what was the due share of the Pandavas. He came to the rescue of Draupadi when her modesty was outraged by Dussasana in the open court of Duryodhana in the full glare of a court full of stupefied courtiers, seers and her helpless husbands. And as the unarmed charioteer of Arjuna, He shook up Arjuna from stupefied inactivity to gallant warfare, gifting the world with the famed Bhagavad Gita on the warfront.

The Yadava tribe, of which He was a member, existed only for thirty six years after the Kurukshetra war. Having finished His life mission, His end was destined to come.

While reposing on a tree top, the big toe of the Lord appeared as the beak of a parrot to a nomadic archer who sent an arrow which was instrumental in the Lord giving up His life.

KALKI

The tenth incarnation of Lord Vishnu

Kalki is the tenth incarnation of Lord Vishnu. Sreemad Bhagavatham describes Kalki thus: Kalki is born to a Brahmin by name Vishnu Yasas of Sambhala Village. He, who is the saviour of the whole Universe possesses the eight riches (Ashtiswaryangal-Anima, Mahima, Lakima, Karima, Esvitvam, Vasithvam, Prapti, Prakamyam), is dazzling and mounting a horse Devadatham exterminates the wicked kings in millions and buzzes past on the galloping horse back across the world. With the incarnation of the Lord as Kalki, the Kali Yuga ends and the Kritha yuga starts.

It should be remembered that Kalki does not appear at the start but at the close of Kali yuga and His appearance is the harbinger of Kali Yuga end and start of Krtha Yuga. The reason is that while the Lord is in the Universe, Kali cannot enter the world and it does so in the absence of the Lord. Obviously Kali should exit with the emergence of the Lord. It is mentioned that the father of Kalki is Vishnu Yasas but His mother is not mentioned. It is not mentioned whether the visage is human and if yes, the gender, for the visage is masked in a visor. Galloping on a horseback, He doesn't pause even and kills Kings in millions. In Kali Yuga, when kings have dwindled to digit numbers, it may seem questionable how kings in millions are exterminated. It may be that the ego of everyone, boosted to the level of delusions King's like is what is aimed at.

Let us remove the human element from the above description. The surf at the sea shore with the surging sea behind, rising tree-high, has the appearance of a galloping white horse and the uprooted trees resemble brandished swords. The body of water following the wave is the great deluge. The description of Kalki thus perfectly fits the Tsunami we had witnessed. Supposing that such an event happened on a mammoth scale and involving the whole world, probably the incarnation of Kalki would, in all probability be enacted. It is not mentioned as to what happens to Kalki. But it is mentioned that with the incarnation of Kalki, Kali Yuga ends and a new Kratha Yuga starts. But in Kritha Yuga, the incarnation of the Lord is as a Fish. Which means the Avtar Kalki is only transcient and devastating and is meant to purge the Universe and is lost as soon as it is formed and what follows is from the seas, namely fish.

7

Chapter

SIGNIFICANCE OF THE INCARNATIONS OF LORD VISHNU

What does the Lord say about His incarnations? The famous quote from The Bhagavad Gita is often used to answer this question. It runs thus:

Yada Yada hi Dharmasya, Glanir bhavathi Bharatha,
Abhyuthanamadharmasya, That atmanam srujamyaham.
Paritranaya sadhoonam Vinasaya cha dushkritham,
Dharmasamsthapanarthaya, Sambhavami yuge, yuge.

(Whenever there is decadence of Dharma and rise of Adhrma, O! Bharatha, I embody myself. To protect the virtuous, for the destruction of the wicked and for the establishment of Dharma, I am born yuga after yuga.)

That a crime should have a punishment commensurate with its magnitude is a dictum which is as old as humanity and handed down to posterity. That is, a good act should not go unrecognized nor a bad act unpunished. And who metes out the justice? When an ordinary mortal commits a crime, the law enforcing machinery springs into action and he is brought to books. And the law enforcing machinery may be a cop, a judge, a legislator, a king, a citizen or one's conscience depending on the time, place or position. This is what the Lord means when He says

"I am born *yuga* after *yuga*." But when the head of a state is bad or corrupt and the law enforcing machinery itself is defective and there is decadence throughout with none to control, it becomes incumbent on the Lord to protect the few, if at all any, virtuous. This is what the Lord means when He asserts "I embody myself." When we examine the incarnations of Lord Vishnu, we understand that this is true in some of the incarnations only. In the *Matsya Avtar,* it was to retrieve the Vedas the *Asura* Hyagreevan stole from the face of Brahmadeva. Here Hyagreeva was slain and the *Vedas* restored to Brahmadeva. At the same time the virtuous king Sathyavrata and the seven sages-*Saptarshis* were protected which goes in line with His professed aim. But in the *Koorma Avatar,* Maha Vishnu incarnated as a tortoise only to extract Amruthu, so that the Devas did not suffer premature senility due to the curse of Sage Durvasa. If this could be considered as protecting the virtuous or punishing the wicked, then the metamorphosis as Mohini by the Lord should be considered as an incarnation of the Lord as much as that of Koorma; for it was as Mohini that the Lord retrieved Amruthu and handed it over to the Devas. But Mohini is not included in the *Dasavatharams* of the Lord. Why? As *Varaha or wild boar, Maha Vishnu retrieved the Earth* hidden by Hiranyakshan in *Pathalam* or the nether world, slaying the wicked *Asura.* As *Narasimham,* the Lord slew Hiranyakasipu, who achieved near immortality from the boon granted by Brahmadeva, and thus emancipating a whole kingdom of disgruntled citizens, ascetics and also a virtuous devotee, Prahlada, from the wicked *Asura.* Mahabali was a King, generous to a fault, who ruled his kingdom to the praise of his subjects and the envy of gods even. Even then the Lord, as *Vamana* chose to push him to the nether world, to uphold which

Dharma? To punish which wicked? And *Parasurama* was Nemesis incarnate. He killed His mother and siblings when asked to do so by His father, little thinking about the righteousness involved in the act. He killed king Karthaveerarjuna and his sons to settle petty scores. And as though to remind that Nemesis has no frontiers, He went on a killing spree, killing any vestige even, of a *Kshathriya* left. *Sree Rama and Sree Krishna* are the two incarnations where the Lord exemplified the meaning of His professed aim. But in the incarnation as *Balarama* the situation is totally different. Balarama was tutor to Duryodhana in the warfare with the maze and thus helped the wicked. Also during the Kurukshetra war when Sree Krishna became Arjuna's charioteer, instead of helping the Pandavas and thus virtuousness, Balarama went on a pilgrimage, thus indirectly helping the wicked. And wicked or virtuous, *Kalki* killed everyone, purging the world in a deluge. Thus only in five incarnations did the Lord help the virtuous and punish the wicked- *Matsya, Varaha, Narasimha, Sree Rama and Sree Krishna.* In the rest of the incarnations, His professed aim is found to be deviated from. So the *Dasavatharams* of the Lord do not actually represent what the Lord says about His incarnations, when taken in the literal sense.

Stories aside, what is the significance of the incarnations of Lord Vishnu? Are they mere myths or fanciful stories created out of the imagination of some one? Maha Vishnu is the Omnipotent, Omnipresent, Omniscient power on the Universe. He has at His disposal all the powers, super natural or otherwise and it is preposterous to believe that He had to assume the form and figure of lowly creatures to attain His goal. Without as much as lifting a finger, He could have erased Hayagreeva and restored the Vedas to Brahmmadeva, prevented the Mandhara Mountain from dropping or retrieved the Earth concealed by Hiranyakshan. He could have chosen different forms of humans than reverting to animal forms. Or, he could have assumed the form of *Vamana* first and fish as last or any of the alternatives possible. And yet He chose none and allowed the way it happened, possibly with a motive.

Let us recapitulate the incarnations of Lord Vishnu :

a.   Matsya – Fish – lives in water.

b.   Koorma- Tortoise- lives in water as well as land.

c.   Varaham-Wild   boar-mammal-aesthetically   a mammal at the lower end but biologically a mammal, all the same.

d.   Narasimham: Torso of lion and hind of man. Represents animal at its royal best, shedding animal nature and trying to become human (a 'sophomore' human)

e.   Vamana- A dwarf Brahmin- man at his small start.

f.   Parasurama- Fully developed man, but angry and immature.

g.   Sree Rama- The human form at its perfect best. No bettering is possible.

h.   Balarama-Demigod- above human and next to God.

i.   Sree Krishna-The perfect incarnation of God. Out and out God.

j.   Kalki- The exterminator- The harbinger of the great deluge which at once exterminates an old order and sets in pace a new one.

A perusal of the incarnations of Lord Vishnu reveals that it is not a bad story, haphazard or badly crafted but crafted by a master craftsman to tell a credible and true story, the way a scientist does with scientific precision. It tells us how organic evolution took place in the Universe.

ORGANIC EVOLUTION

Biologists use the term Organic Evolution to describe the process by which organisms evolved in the Universe. From a humble start as a single celled animal like the amoeba, whose only cell served all bodily functions, evolution went a long way through multi cellular organisms culminating in the creation of man as the acme of creation.

During the process of evolution, the single celled organism gave way to multi cellular organisms (thus bringing in division of labour) encompassing all insects, urchins, worms, flukes and the whole gamut of spineless animals. The cross roads reached when a semblance of a spine began to show (in an animal called amphioxus. It has been said that had amphioxus not been discovered, it would have to have been invented because it typifies a generalized chordate and acts as a connecting link between invertebrates and vertebrates. And then the diversification to vertebrate animals or animals with spine began. Scientists classify such animals with spine thus:

a. Pisces- Fishes- live in water.

b. Amphibia- Frogs, newts etc which can live in land and water.

c. Reptilia- Reptiles which can live in air, water, land etc and their charnacteristic is belly touching the ground in locomotion.

d. Aves- Birds with special adaptation for flight or otherwise.

e. Mammilia- Mammals, characterised by animals giving birth to babies and suckling the young at breast.

It is not mere chance or coincidence that the first incarnation of Vishnu should be Pisces (fishes). Were it so, it could have been any other organism. Or, why for that matter, the second incarnation should be a Tortoise which lives in both land and water (and thus amphibious, though not an amphibian). It may be argued that the tortoise is not an amphibian but is a reptile but then what better way is there to present the Lord as a decent animal than the tortoise, without compromising on specificity and veracity?

Zoologists consider both reptiles and birds as off shoots from the same parent stock and this explains why Vishnu did not incarnate as a bird. In other words, birds could be considered reptiles with flight adaptation. The incarnation next to Koorma or tortoise is Varaha or wild boar, which represents a lowly mammal. Evolutionally mammals also share a common ancestry with reptiles like birds do, as is evidenced from the primitive mammal, the duck billed platypus, which though a mammal shows distinctly reptilian characters.

The Narasimha incarnation represents human in the making and presents the characteristic of both man and the beast. It, again, is an example of a connecting link. A connecting link refers to an animal which by virtue of its characteristic gives a clue as to its descent. Here the beastly nature is giving way to humane form is what Narasimha tells us. There are a few examples of connecting links. For example how animals with a vertebral column or vertebrates evolved from spineless animals or invertebrates is suggested by an animal called Amphioxus. This animal differs from other spineless animals by the presence of a rudimentary spinal cord and differs from full- fledged vertebrates by the absence of a fully developed vertebral column, thus serving as a connecting link between vertebrates and invertebrates. How did birds evolve? Well the clue is offered by an animal called Archaeopteryx. This animal has become long extinct, but a fossil of it was discovered in the lime formations in Bavaria in the year 1939. Its distinctly reptilian characters are the presence of a beak with teeth in it, wings with claws in them suggesting the reptilian nature of upper limbs with claws, the presence of a long tail as in a reptile and unlike in a bird. It is a bird because of the presence of wings. The suggestion that mammals evolved from reptiles gains ground from the clues offered by the Duck billed Platypus, a mammal found in Australia. This animal, like a reptile lays eggs but the young ones are fed at the breast, typically a mammalian trait. It may be argued that the traits mentioned here are subtle and hardly perceptible while *Narasimha* as half lion and half man is easily discernible. The answer is, one is a scientific fact mentioned as such; the other is presented as a folk lore for lay people to understand easily. It should be remembered that the dominant trait in Narasimha is still beastly as the torso is feline and the human form is only beginning to appear.

CONNECTING LINKS

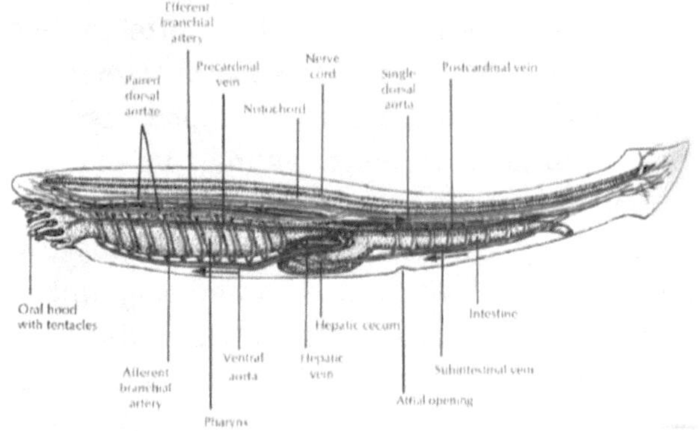

Fig. 1   **AMPHIOXUS** - connecting link between spineless animals (invertebrates) and animals with spine (vertebrates). The appearance is very much fish like, but Amphioxus lacks a fully developed spinal cord and vertebrae which go to make a fish.

Fig. 2   **ARCHAEOPTERYX** - connecting link between reptiles and birds. The wing is avian, but the claw in it is reptilian; the beak is avian, but the teeth in it are reptilian; the long tail is distinctly reptilian.

Fig. 3 **SPINY ANT-EATER (ECHIDNA)** - is a primitive mammal found in Australia and New Guinea. The female lays egg, one in a year and the young one hatching out is kept in a pouch in the belly of the mother and suckles at the breast of the mother. The egg laying trait is reptilian and breast feeding, mammalian.

Fig. 4 **DUCK-BILLED PLATYPUS** - is considered a primitive mammal, connecting reptiles and mammals. While moving, its belly touches the ground, it has webbed feet and lives in burrows. The female lays eggs, one to three and the young ones hatching out live in the burrow for about four months, feeding on mother's milk.

Connecting links are animals, living, dead, extinct or fossilized which by virtue of their anatomic peculiarity offer a possible clue as to how evolution might have progressed. When an animal possesses a trait of an evolutionally higher and a lower class, it is surmised that evolution from a lower to a higher class took place. Let us examine this in a few animals.

From invertebrate to vertebrate: When the single celled organism progressed to multi cellular animals, the long route taken through germs and worms, insects and flukes, mussels and urchins- all spineless animals- finally reached the cross-roads when further progression was possible only with the acquisition of a spine. And the first animal with a spine is fishes. And how the spineless animal progressed to an animal with spine-fish- is illustrated by an animal called Amphioxus (Branchiostoma lanceolatum). This animal looks like a fish and has an anatomy almost like a fish but it lacks a spine. Yet a rudimentary spinal cord called notochord or chorda dorsalis characterizes this animal and hence this animal assumes importance as the first predecessor of fishes. Were it not for the notochord, Amphioxus would have to have been included under the invertebrates (spineless animals) but the absence of a well developed vertebral column precludes it being classified as a vertebrate. Hence it is classified as a distinct entity called chordate and is considered as a connecting link between spineless animals and those with spine.

Fish out of water is a term we often use. Out of water it dies in no time. Acquisition of the ability to live out of water is the first step to a life on land. And before life on land was possible, a period of 'internship' in water and land was in the waiting as an amphibian. And fishes didn't march out as amphibians. First they had a taste of life out of water.

This is what happens in fishes like Anabas scandens and Ophiocephalus. These fishes have accessory respiratory organs, so much so, they can live outside water for hours on end- but not for ever- for that is the prerogative of the amphibians typified in frog, newt etc.

Once animals got the taste of land, they revelled in it. They ran or crawled on the newly opened vistas, they climbed and glided on trees, swam in water and at times attempted to fly. And whatever they did, wherever they hid, their bellies touched the ground, thus getting grouped under reptiles. Reptiles became so dominant that during the period called Mesozoic age they ruled the earth. This age is called "the golden age of reptiles" and it was during this period such gigantic reptiles like Dinosaurs ran the length and breadth of earth.

"Had I wings!" is a thought anyone must have nursed, and poor reptiles might have thought as much. As though partly fulfilling this thought, reptiles did get a "wing" in Draco (the flying lizard). Though it did not compare with the wing of a bird, it helped the lizard in gliding short distances, and is a pointer as to which direction evolution is aiming to progress.

Reptiles represent a milestone in evolution, for they provided the ancestral stock from which birds and mammals evolved. (Animals like the flying fox and the flying squirrel are mammals with "flying ability"- they are actually gliding- and may be mistaken for acquisition of flying ability in mammals). A reptile with wing is a bird. This concept is based on the discovery of the fossil of a bird, the size of a crow, recovered from the lime formations in Bavaria. The bird, Archaeopteryx represents a connecting link between reptiles and birds. Its distinctly reptilian characters are the presence of a long jaw with teeth in it, the wings (which represent the fore-limb of a reptile) with claws in them and a long tail. But it is a bird because of the presence of a fully developed wing.

The reptilian ancestry of mammals is provided by the Duck-billed Platypus, Ornithorhynchus, which is a primitive mammal found in Australia. It has characteristic of both mammals and reptiles. It lives in burrows, and its reptilian characters are the belly touching the ground while moving, the presence of a long tail and webbed feet. It lays eggs but nurses the young at breast making it a mammal, primitive though it be.

Thus Amphioxus, Archaeopteryx and Ornithorhynchus teach us what connecting links are. The Narasimha Avtar represents the transformation from beast to human, as the human form is just getting formed. The Vamana Avtar represents the full fledged human form. But the short stature is meant to suggest that the human form is only just acquired and evolution into a full- fledged human is still far away. And with the incarnation as Parasurama, this lacuna has successfully been patched. But Parasurama is still far from the true human attributes, and is rough with none of the finer humane aspects. This perfection is achieved in the Sree Rama Avatar which represents the fine tuned human with no room left for perfectionism. And further promotion is only as god, namely Sree Krishna with an intervening demigod, Balarama. Balarama represents the start of the deification process. And having reached the stage of god, nothing more remains and the next stage is setting the stage ready for a new order and this cleaning role is relegated to Kalki.

8

Chapter

THE TRIMURTIS – MAHADEVA

Variously named Parameswaran, Paramasivaan, Maheswaran, Sivan, Neeelakantan, Mahadevan and the like, Mahadeva represents the second syllable U (pronounced–oo-) in Omkara or Pranava Mantra. He is the personification of death and His visage marks death in its stark reality including the various ways in which death is possible. The tuft of hair in His head lodges Ganga (the Ganges) meaning death by water or drowning. He derives the name Gangadharan from this. Lord Siva has a name Chandrakaladharan derived from the crescent he wears on the tuft of hair. The lunacy in man next only to death is the idea behind hoisting the crescent to the Godhead.

The courting by Parvathy of Paramasiva is a long and arduous story of penance and sacrifice. Parvathy in her endeavour to obtain Siva as her husband was helped by Kamadeva (God of love), who, in a moment of ill wit, shot His arrow of flowers (called the Sammohan astra) at Paramasiva doing penance. Enamoured and broken of His penance, Paramasiva courts Parvathy, but soon realising the cause for His subjugation burns Kamadeva to ashes. The third eye of Paramasiva in the middle of His forehead provided the fire to burn Him.

Two serpents adorn the countenance of Paramasiva. The one around his neck denotes death by hanging (the serpent represents the rope in hanging) and the coils of the snake represent death by strangulation. (Try to hold your neck with your hand like in strangulation and you will notice that while the thumb looks like the hood of a serpent, the encircling fingers take after the coils of the serpent). The second snake worn on His upper arm denotes death by snake bite. Paramasivan is known by various other names, one of which is Neelakantan or the one with a blue neck, and hence is a reference to death by consumed poison.

For a weapon, Paramasiva wields a trident and hence signifies death by weapons. The loin cloth of Paramasiva is made of tiger hide meant to represent death by wild animals. The four hands of Paramasiva hold, a trident in one hand, the damaru or small drum in the second, Yogadandu in the third and Kamandalu in the fourth. The yogadandu has the appearance similar to the thigh bone (femur) and arm bone (humerus). It is not evident what the kamandalu (vessel) holds, but going by the look of things, it ought to contain blood. The sound from the 'Damaru' has a peculiar unearthly and almost eerie overtone and emanates decibels of melancholy.

In addition to the various ways in which death is possible is being depicted in the visage of Paramasiva, manifestations of death are writ large on the body of the Lord. The ash from funeral pyre smeared all over the body and the garland of human skull are examples. Even the Siva Thandavam or the dance of death that Paramasiva performs spells devastation and probably represents the last struggle of a dying person.

The mathematical precision in the pictorial representation of Paramasiva is seen in the description of His abode as well. Paramasiva inhabits the snow clad peak of the Himalayas (the peak of the world is 29000 feet above the mean sea level) where life comes to a standstill. (20000 feet

Lord Shiva as Death Personified Form

Lord Shiva as Ardhanareeswaran

Shiva Lingam

above mean sea level is the highest altitude possible for permanent human habitation attained with acclimatization spanning weeks). At a height of twenty five thousand feet life becomes critical. The temperature goes below -30 degrees, the atmospheric pressure falls and these result in a low partial pressure of oxygen in the blood. At low pressure, the volume of all gases increases. Because of the low oxygen content in the blood, blood oozes out of the capillaries in the alveoli of the lungs. Rupture of the capillaries in the nose results in nasal bleeding. A whole lot of internal changes may lead to death. Thus the abode of Paramasiva also smacks of death.

Death is a proposition few people are willing to accept. The reluctance on the part of people to worship a God, who from head to toe symbolises death, is understandable. Thus no one worships Mahadeva in His fully embellished, death personified form. In its stead Siva Lingam which symbolises procreation is worshipped; or Siva along with Parvathy as Ardhanareeswara find place in the worship of devotees -the cadaveric countenance balanced with the exquisite feminine beauty and vivacity.

Worship of God is the delight of any devotee. But in the case of Lord Siva even this is minced with reluctance. Devotees of any God usually complete one or three circles in circum ambulation around their deity as a mark of respect and this is always through the right of the deity- called Pradakshinam, never the other way round. But the devotees of Paramasiva make a pradakshinam of half a circle through the right, immediately reverting to apradakshinam or circumambulation anti-clock wise for the rest of the circle. While pradakshinam is meant to give respect, apradakshinam takes away any respect already given.

Nor does this respectful disrespect stop there. While every deity is worshipped after lighting the oil lamp in front, in case of Paramasiva what is specially offered is 'Pin Vilakku' or lamp lit from the back. What, if a soldier salutes his big wigs on the arse, instead of on the forehead!

PARAPHERNALIA OF PARAMASIVA

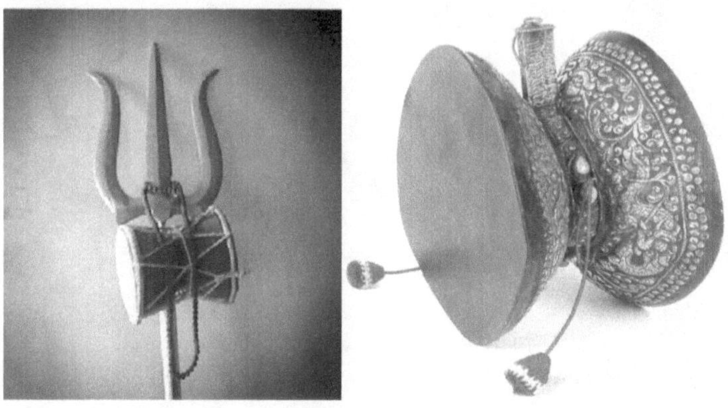

Trident (trisul)   Damaru

Skull necklace

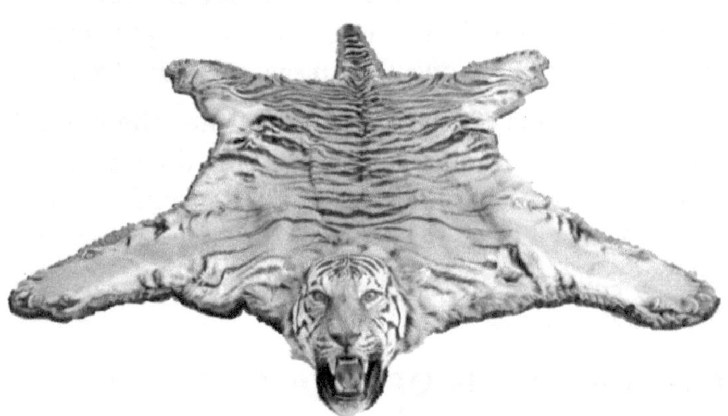

Tiger hide

Kamandalu   **Yogadhandu**

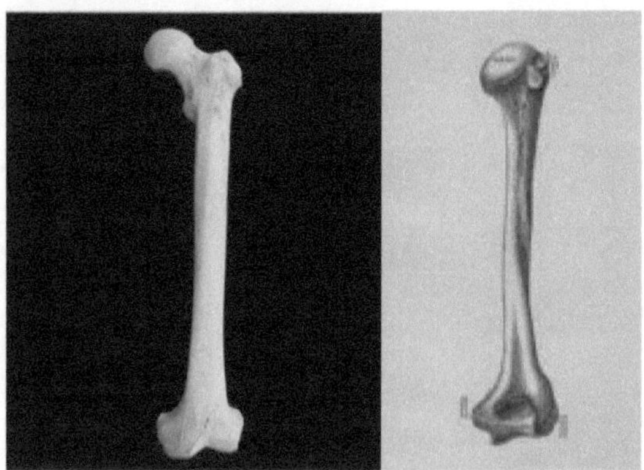

The yogadhandu of sri Parameswaran compared with the thigh and arm bones of humans. Note how perfectly it compares.

Nataraja or the dancing shiva. The dance of shiva is called shiva thandavam and always spells devastation. It may be presumed that shiva thandavam spells the last struggle of a dying person.

THE MAHAVAKYAS

Mahvakyas are great quotations derived one from each Veda and contained in the Upanishads. We have four of them and these are:

Prajnanam Brahmam - Aithereya Upanishad of Rig Veda.

Ayamatma Brahmam - Mandukya Upanishad of Atharva Veda.

Tat Tvam Asi - Chandogya Upanishad of Sama Veda and

Aham Brahmasmi - Brihadaranyaka Upanishad of Yajur Veda.

PRAJNANAM BRAHMAM

Prajna is Brahmam. This Mahvakya is contained in the Aithareya Upanishad of Rig Veda. What is Prajna? The Aithareyopanishad lists what all constitute Prajna:

Samjnanam - comprehensive knowledge.

Aajnanam - Is commanding power. It is considered a divine trait.

Vijnanam - knowledge of what is best in materialistic pursuits

Prajnanam - Bliss of knowledge.

Medha - comprehensive reading.

Drishti - interpret what is seen by eyes.

Drithi-Courage - It is the ability to overcome mental and body fatigue.

Mathi - thought.

Maneesha - Freedom of thought.

Joothi - Is mental depression in disease or disaster.

Smruthi - Mental recollection.

Sankalpa - Is the ability to discriminate form as black, white etc.

Kruthu - determination.

Asu - what determines life support like respiration etc.

Kama - Is to aspire for lust beyond one's means. *Vasam*-Is desire for company of women.

All the above mentioned faculties are called higher cortical functions meaning they are the functions of the cerebral cortex. The human brain has a cerebrum formed of two hemispheres, a cerebellum, again formed of two hemispheres and medulla oblongata. Each half of the cerebral hemisphere is divided into a sensory and a motor cortex. The motor cortex is concerned with the control of muscular activities and the sensory cortex is concerned with the appreciation of the various sensations.

To understand where the brain comes into play, it is necessary to understand how the sensations are appreciated. Each sensation has what is called a sensory pathway, which consists of sensory receptors, first order neurons, second order neurons a sensory relay station, third order neurons and finally the cerebral cortex.

For appreciating a sense, say sight, the receptors are the rods and cones situated in the retina of the eyeball. The first order neurons are in the eyeball, so also the second order neurons which come out of the eyeball as the Optic Nerve, cross over to the opposite side and relay in the relay station situated in the brain called the lateral geniculate body. From here, third order neurons sweep and reach the cerebral cortex where interpretation of the sensation takes place. That is, though we see with the eyes, what we actually see is interpreted only in the cerebral cortex and for sight, this area is in the occipital lobe of the cerebral cortex.

Having spoken about what Prajnanam is, the third Mantra of the Aithareya Upanishad (chapter III) dwells on the relation between Prajnanam and Brahmam. It says that ***Brahmam is Atma manifesting as Prajnanam.*** Indra and Prajapathi are Atma. All Gods are Atma. Earth, Air, Sky, Water and Fire which form the Pancahbhootha, all animals whether born of egg, from mother's womb, born out of sweat, or splitting the earth, all those living things however small and in all denominations, horses, humans, elephants and all things which move or fly and all things immobile are led by Prajnanam and are rooted in Prajnanam. The whole world is led by Prajna. Prajna is the refuge of all. Prajnanam is Brahmam.

We have seen that Prajna encompasses a huge list of human endeavour, the finer aspects of life, animate and inanimate objects and so on and all these are modulated by the brain. Thus whatever activity one does, imagines or thinks has its root in the brain. Scientists have located specific areas in the brain responsible for all these. For example what is called the limbic system in the brain has functions like sensing smell, regulation of endocrine system which controls many of the body functions, regulation of heart rate, blood pressure, water balance, body temperature, regulation of food intake, regulation of sleep, wakefulness, regulation of sexual function, emotional state, motivation etc. Another area in the brain called the reticular formation is concerned with wakefulness, alertness, control of voluntary and reflex movements etc. Thus whatever be the exploits of man (Atma), whether translated as thoughts or transformed into actions, have their roots in Prajna (Brain).

One may be tempted to argue how man with such a fully developed brain with all activities marked in different areas of the brain compare with a worm or an insect with no brain, or if at all, with a poorly developed or imperfectly developed brain. Or, for that matter, a stone or steel with no life, leave alone brain equate with the brain of a man? For, according to the concept Prajnanam is Brahmam, any organism however small or insignificant or any object animate or inanimate has Prajnanam and is guided by Prajna. Let us find out.

Anyone who has seen a rat would be provoked by its insolence. It jumps, sometimes at you, at times biting, anyway hiding with all your attempts at outsmarting it failing. You try poison; it does not fall for it. And the moment you set a trap, the rat menace stops. It doesn't trap the rat, the rat moves to safer pastures.

Have you seen the labour room of rats? I have seen many. In a plantain bunch, between two rows of plantains, rats stuff hay or leaves and make a comfy cushion and into this the rat delivers its babies, protected by the warmth and beyond the gaze of hungry predators. And yet, a snake crawls seeking the rat, at whose beckoning?

You open your kitchen and cockroaches buzz past, many a time giving you the creeps-at times creeping all over your body. You count them-their number defies counting. Try hitting one-you won't kill one but the next moment the rest of them goes into hiding. You try Lakshmana Rekha-you may kill a few, but the rest escape.

And who gave these lowly animals or insects the power to escape from their enemies? This is Prajnanam.

Even before Scientists found out that plants have life-that may be a couple of hundred years-mention of the presence of life in plants is detailed in the Aithereya upanishad of Rig Veda and the Chandogya Upanishad of Sama veda, believed to have originated ten thousand years back. Yet, it may be difficult to believe that plants have brain. Take a seed and plant it with the notch facing up, down or any manner you like- the seedling which sprouts always comes up splitting the soil; and the stem comes up and the roots go down. Who instructed them thus?

Plant a seedling in the shade, well protected from the scorching Sun, water it, tend to it. You note that as the seedling grows into a tree, it bends, shunning the shade and following light. Scientists call this phototropism, but who gave them the brain to do this? This is Prajnanam.

We have seen the roots of plants piercing buildings even, in search of water. Why didn't they stay where they were and let the plant perish? This is called Asu, the instinct to support life and is Prajnanam.

A primitive plant like Spirogyra, constituted only of filaments, with no semblance of a brain, shows the like of sexual reproduction by a process of conjugation. And who gave these brainless plants the sexual urge? This is vasam or kamam and is Prajna.

Which is all well with living things, but how do we account for Prajna in non living things like stone, mountain, seas etc.? We have seen Tsunami strike. What if it happened on a daily basis? Who gave the water in the ocean the instruction not to do it often? The mountains do not come crashing down, but stay where they are: At whose behest? The stones do not rub against each other and cause fire, though they could: Why? Marsh gas is constantly being produced in marshy places, from cow dung etc and these are combustible gases and the oxygen in the atmospheric air aids combustion. A spark anywhere from any source should theoretically ignite the whole world in an inferno, but it hardly ever does. Why?

The Panchabhoothas- Earth, Air, Water, Sky and Fire are also guided by Prajna. The earth does not cave in, the air does not strike as whirl wind, cyclone etc, the sky does not come down, water in the river limits itself to the banks and fire does not become an inferno when a candle is lit. It is as though a discipline is enforced to prevent such natural calamities or in other words it looks as though a little brain is put in all living and non living things to keep the world disciplined. What happens when this discipline is broken is occasionally shown to us in the form of natural calamities, idiosyncrasies in animal behaviour etc.

AHAM BRAHMASMI

Is a Mahavakya quoted from the Brihadaranyaka Upanishad of Yajur Veda. The text in which this Mahavakya appears reads thus: "The Atma situated in the body was Brahmam even before. But when it recognized itself "I am Brahmam" it became all pervasive. Hence, whoever among the Gods knew the Atma as Brahmam, he alone became the omnipresent Brahmam. This applies to the Rishis and humans as well. The Rishi Vamadevan who achieved this supreme knowledge became enlightened thus realising "I am Manu, I am the Sun God." Even now whoever recognizes Brahmam in the Atma, he becomes all of this. Nobody, not even the Gods become competent to prevent his all pervasiveness, because he is their Atma as well. Whoever seeks a God outside of self is far from the truth. Thus ill informed one is like milch cow to the Gods. Like a herd of cows serves one master, so also each such un-enlightened man serves many a God. When one cow is preyed upon by a tiger, the loss is accounted much. Imagine one's plight when many such cows are lost. So man's self realisation is not welcomed by the Gods."

This is one of the greatest Mahavakyas of all times. Just like Mohammed Ali claiming "I am the greatest, I am the prettiest," how does realising "I am Brahmam" help anyone become great? It is said that the Atma situated in the body was Brahmam even before, but realisation of this fact made him great. We have heard many people exclaim "What a fool I was!" For example in chess you make a move and in the next moment your opponent check-mates you taking advantage of your wrong move and you exclaim "What a fool I was!" (to have committed that move). It means that you were a fool at the time of committing the mistake but realisation that you were a fool dawned on you later. Had you known that the move you were going to make would be a folly and be fatal, you would not have made the move. That means realisation of your mistake was possible only when you became wiser. Not only when one had made a mistake, even otherwise, the strength of a man depends on the knowledge of the strength and weaknesses of his vis-a-vis his adversary's. In the same way the Atma situated in the body was Brahmam but realisation by the Atma that it was Brahmam came only later. There are two aspects: one is the knowledge that the Atma is Brahmam is realised by the Atma which hitherto had not realized this. This is because of the acquisition of knowledge. Secondly the intelligence which makes practical use of this knowledge. The Atma which recognizes itself as Brahmam would not stoop before anybody for any bounty because what bounty he seeks from elsewhere is available with himself-only he has to strive for it. In other words it means self-confidence. A man with self confidence can attain any height and not bow before anybody and does not crave for favours from anybody.

The averment that the Gods would not be able to offer him any hindrance is the extreme extent to which self confidence could be boosted. In the Vedic times, Gods meant the natural forces man worshipped like wind, fire, water, lightning etc. A man with self confidence could conquer the world come what may-towering infernos, mad showers, wild tempests or rising Tsunami.

The assertion that Gods prefer the ignorant to the enlightened because only the former perform yajnas by which the Gods get their food and the enlightened ones because they perform no yajnas deprive the Gods of their food is again an exposition of the plight of the enlightened. The enlightened one would not spend time and energy for any gain, material or spiritual because he knows that the very Gods he worships to appease, have the same

Brahmam he also possesses and hence it would be an exercise in futility performing yajnas. Instead, he spends the time and energy to acquire whatever he wanted, not by appeasement and worship but by work derived from knowledge.

AYAM ATMA BRAHMA

This mahavakya is from the Mandukya Upanishad of Atarva Veda. The text runs thus:

Sarvam hyedad Brahma, Ayam Atma Brahma,
Soyamatma chathushpad.

(All that has been said before (as AUM) applies to Brahmam. This atma is also Brahmam. That Atma and this Atma have four existences.)

To understand what the second mantra is, it is necessary to understand what the first mantra means:

AUM ithyed aksharam idam sarvam, thasyopa vyakyanam,
Bhootahm, bhavad, bhavyshad iti, sarvam AUMkara eva.
Yatchanyad trikala atheetam that api AUM kara eva.

(Whatever is seen is AUM. Its most lucid explanation is thus: past, present or future anything which existed, exists or would exist are all AUM. Whatever has transgressed the three tenses is also AUM.)

The second mantra of the Mandukya Upanishad relegates the same status to Brahmam. In addition, this Atma (pointing to the heart) which kindles in all lives is also Brahmam. The first mantra of the Mandukya Upanishad tells about AUM. Having said that what existed in the past, exists now and is to happen hence and what transgresses time, and space is AUM, the same attribute is said to be what qualifies Brahmam. Apart from that, this Atma inside all-the antharyami-is also Brahmam. What is significant here is the use of the term Ayamatma Brahma meaning this Atma is also Brahmam (pointing to the Atma inside of self). Having said that everything is Brahmam, it may seem rather superfluous to tell that this Atma is also Brahmam. When a teacher tells that all the students in her class have English texts and adds that John also has one, it either means that John is not a regular student of the class or that John is habituated in doing things different from the rest of the class. That is, John has an identity different from the rest of the class. Here this Atma (Ayamatma) is emphasised because it has a definite function namely equate with the other Brahmam while maintaining a separate identity. The idea is to show two separate identities and then prove that both are the same. In other words the Advaitha philosophy is what is aimed at. When one looks at the world, two entities are involved: one the person who sees and the other, what is looked at (the Atmas which are seen.) And when the next line is recited, it is to tell that both are the same and have the same four existences.

We can see a subtle difference between the Atma (Brahmam) inside (Antharyami) and the Atma (Brahmam) outside. The Brahmam inside is non materialistic (invisible) while the Brahmam outside is material (visible) and pervades the universe. This could be more easily understood by analysing the whole thing scientifically. We have oft repeated that any object in the universe, living or non living, atom small or mountain big has two constituents namely matter and energy. While the term

Brahmam denotes the materialistic nature in the universe, the term AUM denotes the energy aspect of Brahmam-that which remains unseen.

TAT – TVAM – ASI

Is a Mahavakya derived from the Chandogya Upanishad of Sama Veda. It means "That thou art." The full text reads thus:

Sa ya eshonam ithatatmam idam sarvam

That sathyam sa Atma Tat-Tvam-Asi Svetaketo iti

(The infinitesimally minute aspect or core is the atma of the whole Universe. That alone is the truth and the Atma of all, O! Svetaketu, That thou art.)

Before the genesis of the Universe, before the Universe came to be diversified into its many and varied form, there existed only one thing-Sat- which was the unique and absolute truth. It then diversified and begot its many and variegated form but each had as its core, Sat. Hence Sat is the Atma of the whole Universe.

This quotation from the Chandogya Upanishad of Sama Veda is a dialogue between Uddalaka and his son Svetaketu. Svetaketu at age twelve left home for his Gurukula system of education and returned at age twenty four, after completing his study of the Vedas. He was arrogant that he had mastered the Vedas and hence knew all that were to be known and there remained little to be learnt. Uddalaka was dismayed that his son should be arrogant and haughty instead of being humble, as education ought to have made him. Hence he decides to enlighten Svetaketu. He approaches Svetaketu and converses with him, always addressing him as O! Sowmya (O! the gentle one). He asked his son whether his teacher had not taught him of that by which the unheard becomes heard, the unimagined becomes imagined and the unknown becomes known. Svetaketu asked: "What instruction was that?" Uddalaka replied: "O! Sowmya, if you know clay, you know of all things made of clay. Only clay is the truth; all others are verbal expressions. O! Sowmya, knowing gold makes known all that are made of gold. Only gold is the truth; all others are verbal expressions. O! Sowmya, knowing a nail cutter made of iron makes known all things made of iron; what is true is iron and all other things are verbal expressions."

Svetaketu was baffled. "Truly, my revered teachers would have no knowledge of this. Had they, they surely would have taught me." So he implored Uddalaka to teach him. "Be it so." Uddalaka agreed and step by step he initiates Svetaketu into self realisation and realisation of Brahmam.

Uddalaka taught Svetaketu that Sat decided to diversify and metamorphose and thus got successively transformed into Thejus, App and Annam and these by further successive transformations the universe as we see today evolved. Hence any object in the universe has sat as its core. (We have seen that any object in the universe, living or non living, however small or however big, has two constituents namely matter and energy. And whether matter or energy, they represent atom in the elemental or ionic state. They thus form the core of all objects in the universe.)

When Uddalaka taught Svetaketu that Sat which is the core or Atma which manifests in all objects in the Universe, which alone is the truth and which alone is the Atma of the whole Universe and that was Suetaketu, Svetaketu sought more clarification on this. "Be it so" Uddalaka agreed and continued: "O! Sowmya, just as bees collect nectar from different flowers and convert them into honey, and honey how once formed, the individual nectars lose their identity, so also the different lives unified in the same Sat fail to understand that they are from the same Sat."

"And whatever they were in this world, let them be tiger, lion, wolf, boar, vermin, insect, fly, mosquito, they return like that."

"And the infinitesimally minute aspect or core is the Atma of the whole Universe. That alone is the truth and the Atma of all, O! Svetaketu, That thou art."

"Enlighten me a little more, O! revered one" Svetaketu implored.

"Be it so"Uddalaka replied.(When Svetaketu asked Uddalaka to be more clear, what he implied was that when one goes to sleep in the house and on waking up goes to another house still knows that he had come from the previous house, why was it that animals failed to realize that they all had come from the same Sat when they moved from the body and returned.)

"O! Sowmya, The Ganges and rivers in the East flow eastward. The Indus and rivers in the west flow westward. They flow as river formed from the evaporation of water from the sea. They again flow to merge in the sea from which they formed but do not realize that "I am from such and such river."In the same way, all lives, though formed from the same Sat fail to realise that they are from the same Sat. Whatever they were in this world- tiger, lion, wolf, boar, vermin, insect, fly or mosquito, they return as such."

"And the infinitesimally minute aspect or core is the Atma of the whole Universe. That alone is the truth and the Atma of all, O! Svetaketu, That thou art."

"Enlighten me a little more, O revered one!" Svetaketu implored.

"Be it so." Uddalaka replied.

"O! Sowmya, if someone cuts the base of this big tree, the tree does not wither but exudes gum from the cut site, the same way it does, were the cut in the middle or at the top. And this tree lives happy content at getting its nutrients from the soil.

"If life deserts one branch of this tree, that branch withers. If a second branch is bereft of life that also withers as happens to a third branch and when life leaves the whole tree, the entire tree withers.

O! Sowmya, likewise body bereft of life is dead; not life. And the infinitesimally minute aspect or core is the Atma of the whole Universe. That alone is the truth and the Atma of all, O! Svetaketu, That thou art."

"Enlighten me a little more, O! revered one !" Svetaketu implored.

"Be it so"Uddalaka replied. Uddalaka asked Svetaketu to bring a fruit of the fig tree. "Here it is," Svetaketu replied.

"split it."Uddalaka implored him.

"I have split it, Bhagwan" Svetaketu replied.

"What do you see here?"

"Minute seeds, Bhagwan"

"Valsa, Cut one" Uddalaka asked him.

"I have cut, Bhagwan." Svetaketu replied.

"What do you see?"

"Nothing."

His father told Svetaketu:"O! Sowmya, though you see nothing inside this seed, there is hidden in it a minute part which can grow and develop into a big fig tree. Dearest, note this carefully."

"The infinitesimally minute aspect or core is the Atma of the whole Universe. That alone is the truth and the Atma of all, O! Svetaketu, That thou art."

"Enlighten me a little more, O! revered." Svetaketu implored.

"Be it so." His father replied. (What Svetaketu wanted to be clarified with example was that, if Sat is the proximate cause of this Universe, why is it not overtly possible to understand this.)

"Put this lump of salt in water and bring it to me tomorrow" Uddalaka instructed Svetaketu. Svetaketu did as instructed. "Bring the lump of salt you put in water yesterday." His father asked Svetaketu. Svetaketu searched for but could not find what he looked for.

Because, the salt had dissolved in water. "Taste the water at the top." Uddalaka instructed Svetaketu."Tastes salty" Svetaketu replied. "Take a little water from the middle and taste." "Tastes salty" Svetaketu replied. "Now take a little water from the bottom and taste."

"Tastes salty." Svetaketu replied. "Now pour the water out and come near me."

"The salt you put in the water is still there. Though you cannot see it, you can assume its presence by other means. By the same token, though you cannot see Sat in the body you can assume its presence by other means."

"The infinitesimally minute aspect or core is the Atma of the whole Universe. That alone is the truth and the Atma of all, O! Svetaketu, That thou art."

"Please enlighten me a little more, O! revered" Svetaketu implored.

"Be it so, O! Sowmya" Uddalaka replied.(When Uddalaka said that Sat could be known by other means just as salt is known by tasting, Svetaketu wanted to know what those other means were).

"O! Sowmya, like how a person blind folded and brought from Gandhara Desa and abandoned at a deserted place turns east, north, south or west and laments "I am blind folded and brought and abandoned blindfolded,"

"like how his blind fold was untied and someone directed him "go this way to Gandharam," and how he using his intelligence and knowledge seeks his way village after village and reaches Gandharam, so a person with a teacher knows that his waiting is only till the body is left and once the body is left, he merges with Sat."

"The infinitesimally minute aspect or core is the Atma of the whole Unverse. That alone is the truth and the the Ama of all, O! Svetaketu, That thou art."

"Please enlighten me a little more, O revered!" Svetaketu implored.

"Be it so, O! Sowmya" Uddalaka replied.

"O! Sowmya, relatives gather around a person ill and moribund and question "Do you recognize me, do you recognize me." Till his word unifies in mind, mind in Prana and Prana in the Supreme, he recognizes them."

"When his word unifies in mind, mind in Prana and Prana in Thejus and Thejus in The Supreme, he recognizes them not." This is the penultimate state- the stage between conscience and death or coma. Here no words are spoken, mind does not function, they having merged into prana, meaning only breathing is present. And prana is about to unify in the supreme, meaning the person is about to die and death sets in when the prana has unified in the supreme. "The infinitesimally minute aspect or core is the Atma of the whole Universe. That alone is the truth, and the Atma of all, O! Svetaketu and That thou art."

"Please enlighten me a little more, O! revered!" Svetaketu implored.

"Be it so, O! Sowmya" Uddalaka replied.(If the enlightened and the non enlightened unify in Sat, why the enlightened do not and the non enlightened do repeat may be clarified by an example, is what Svetaketu implores)

"O! Sowmya, King's guards bring a thief, hands tied. "He stole money, he is a thief. Keep red hot iron ready for him," they say. If he has really stolen, he is a thief. Shroud in his lies, he holds the red hot iron, gets burnt and punished."

"If really he has not stolen, he is honest. Shroud in his honesty he holds the red hot iron but he doesn't get burnt and gets released."

"Like how he did not get burnt, the enlightened one does not get reborn. The infinitesimally minute aspect or core is the Atma of the whole Universe. That alone is the truth and the Atma of all, O! Svetaketu and That thou art." And Svetaketu understood his father's words.

The moment a child learns how to stand on its two legs, it simultaneously acquires one more knowledge- how to defy its parents and elders. And over the years, he perfects this knowledge. It is a universal fact that children and youth would trust their friends more than anyone else and expect their teachers to know more than their parents. Thus when Svetaketu returned after his Gurukula teaching, he had reason to be arrogant that he had mastered all that was there to know since he had mastered the Vedas and had his coaching under a Guru. Uddalaka was dismayed at his son's arrogance and wanted to correct him. This he achieves through two means. First, he makes known to his son that what knowledge he had acquired from his teacher was incomplete. And with many examples he leads him to self realisation. If the aim of Uddalaka was to make known to Svetaketu that the Atma in all objects is one and the same, he need not have told Svetaketu the way it was told to him, but to have pointed out to him that the Atma in all was the same, which means he had other designs as well. In singling out Svetaketu as the repository of Sat, what Uddalaka aimed at is evident- he wanted the youth to accept the superiority in others. When such a great soul as his father says that Sat is Svetaketu, and not as you, Svetaketu and me, naturally the youth should be awed by his father's humility. When someone compliments you "You are great," you take it as a formal compliment like "thanks" or "good morning" without attaching any great meaning to it. Repeated the second time, you begin to suspect whether the guy wants something out of you. But oft repeated with no malice or ego, or want, but with due humility, you begin to respect the other for being so considerate. This ability to recognize another's superiority demands one quality called magnanimity. This Uddalaka demonstrated by his own words- of addressing Svetaketu as O! Sowmya - and reminding him that the Atma was the core and it was Svetaketu.

Uddalaka taught Svetaketu that "the Universe as we see it today in its many and variegated form was, at the beginning (of creation) the only one and without alternate Sat. Sat desired that it should diversify and this resulted in its acquisition of the multitudinous forms we see today." Thus in any object in the Universe, living or non living, the presence of Sat is manifest.(This concept has been beautifully expressed in the term Ekatma pratyaya saram mentioned elsewhere. This term means that the Atma present in every object is one and the same or in other words there is no alternate for the Atma.)

That it is so might have been easy for Svetaketu to follow, but what of ordinary mortals like us? Let us examine what all these mean. During the long and arduous process of Organic Evolution, the first organisms to appear were on water and the starting point was a single celled animal typified in amoeba. An amoeba has a single cell and since not comparable to the single cell of a multi cellular organism it is called an a-cellular animal. The single cell of the amoeba divides by a process of binary fission into two amoebae or by multiple fission into a number of amoebae. The nucleus divides first into two, followed by the division of the cytoplasm into two. Thus two identical amoebae are produced.

As evolution progressed, multi cellular organisms (organisms with more than one cell) began to form and the original mode of reproduction by binary fission was replaced by the sexual method, wherein specialized reproductive cells called gametes united and produced a zygote which developed into a new individual. The original method of cell division was retained in other cells of the body.

Thus, whether in the single celled amoeba or in multi cellular organisms, the starting point in the formation of cell or an individual is the division of the nucleus of the cell and once nuclear division is completed, division of the cytoplasm occurs, resulting in the formation of a new cell, which leads us to the conclusion that the nucleus is the all important structure in the cell.

So what is a nucleus? A nucleus is a rounded ball like structure in the centre of the cell, at times in the periphery. It is found to contain a number of filaments which lie coiled and entwined. These are called the chromosomes. The number of chromosomes in each and every single cell in the body is constant (except the gametes, which contain half the number of chromosomes in other cells in the body). In humans it is twenty three pairs of chromosomes. Of the twenty three pairs, twenty two pairs are called autosomes and the remaining one pair is called the sex chromosome. The chromosome pattern, if xx it denotes a female and if xy it denotes a male.

Chromosomes carry the genetic material of an individual called the genes. The genes are carried in the DNA of the chromosomes. Colour of the hair, whether blonde, brunette or black, colour of the eyes, stature of an individual, whether tall or short are all determined by the genes situated in the chromosomes of the individual and are carried over generations.

Thus the genes determine the genetic trait of an individual and are carried in the DNA. And how are they carried?

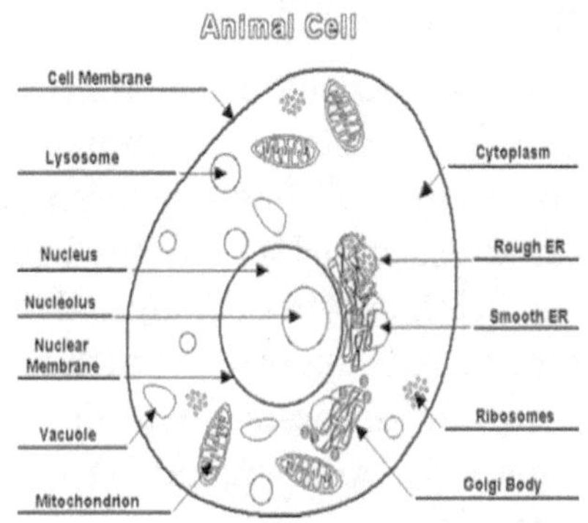

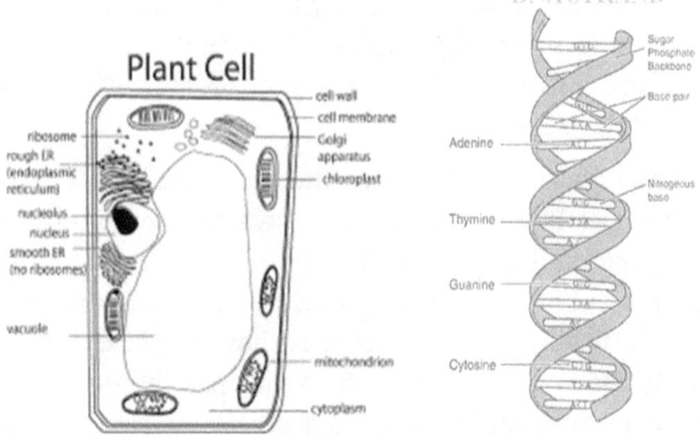

The DNA (Deoxy ribo Nucleic Acid) is a double stranded helical structure with the two strands twisted round each other and running anti parallel. The two strands are poly nucleotides formed of simpler units called nucleotides. Each nucleotide has a nucleo base, which nay either be cytosine or guanine, adenine or thiamine; a sugar deoxy ribose and a phosphate group. The nucleotides are joined to one another, the sugar of one nucleotide joining with the phosphate of the other. The base pairing is between adenine - thiamine and cytosine - guanine. It is the sequence of these nucleo bases which determines the genetic behaviour of animals.

So now we come to the know that from a single celled animal like amoeba to complex creations in nature, plant or animal, all have in common one thing- the chromosomes contained in the nucleus. And while their number determines what the animal or plant is, the disposition of the genetic material (sequence of the nucleo bases) accounts for the differences within the same group of animals- whether a man should be black or white, blonde or brunette etc.

The infinitesimally minute aspect or core is the Atma of the whole universe. The gene carried in the chromosome is the infinitesimally minute aspect or core. This is the Atma of the whole universe.

Thus matter in the elemental form has atoms as the infinitesimally minute aspect or core, energy manifested as an electrical spark has ions (which are atoms with a charge) as the infinitesimally minute aspect or core, while living beings of any denomination have the DNA and the genetic code contained in it as the infinitesimally minute aspect or core. And why should all be the same, if they have not come from the same Sat?

10
Chapter

LIFE AFTER DEATH
(Birth-death-rebirth cycle)

One of the tenets of Hinduism is the belief in rebirth after death of every organism. Human life is considered the ultimate in creation and is attained after countless lives as vermin, insects and other forms of life. Every living being has an outer form or body and an inner soul or Atma and only the body perishes after death while the soul being immortal moves into another body. The deliverance from this cycle is the aim of every form of life and its attainment is called 'Nirvana' or 'Moksha'. This in essence is the concept of rebirth.

Taking a human being as a model, let us examine what happens to the body after death: The body after death is no longer under the control of the individual and the relatives or others may dispose of the body by one of the following or other means.

When the dead is a VIP, the body may be kept for public moaning and cremated with full official honours. In the yester years, when the king or queen demised, they were buried in sandal wood pyres. But for the lay populace, recourse to wood, cow dung cakes, gas or burning in an electric crematorium are the options. Among Christians and Muslims, the dead are not burnt, but kept in a coffin and buried. Certain Hindus are buried while others who claim saint hood are kept in a 'samadhi' (choosing death by volition). Zorastrians are said to leave the dead at the "Tower of silence" for vultures to feed. In ancient Egypt, deceased monarchs were preserved as 'mummies' in the Pyramids.

When the body is burnt, it crumples to ash and partly burnt bone, may be. Part of it goes into the atmosphere as gases like carbon dioxide, water vapour etc. The carbon dioxide and water vapour may be absorbed by plants and the absorbed carbon in the presence of sunlight and water is converted to glucose by plants with chlorophyll by a process called photosynthesis. The carbohydrate so synthesised goes to increase the bulk of the plant or may be converted to fruits, leaves, nuts and flowers. Thus for the body burnt, probably an equal mass is formed as other forms of life. The ash and bone are absorbed by plants as their elements namely potassium sodium, magnesium, zinc, iron calcium etc.

When the body is not burnt, but is left buried or unburied, it decomposes. Decomposition is brought about by bacterial action and starts within a couple of hours after death, unless kept in cold storage. Maggots may feed on the decomposed body, thus increasing their bulk, the gases formed as a result of putrefaction may escape into the atmosphere, the body fluids may seep into the soil as elements and may be absorbed by plants or consumed by animals and humans in the drinking water. Thus the decomposed body also supports many forms of life. Only the skeleton is left behind which takes a long time to crumple down as calcium and mix with the earthly elements.

When preserved as Mummies, the reported change is a slight shrinkage in the size of the body due to loss of water and shrinkage of muscle mass. This is to a large extent compensated by the extraneous agents used in the mummification process; so the total mass remains more or less the same. When the body is left to be fed by birds or animals, it directly contributes to the increase in muscle mass of the animal feeding the carcass.

What we observe from the above is that the death of a person or any living thing does not bring about a total annihilation of the body but a diversion of the body mass into other forms of mass or matter as leaves, fruits, nuts, wood or animals. This leads us to the important Law in Physics namely the Law of conservation of Mass. This law states that mass (matter) can neither be created nor be destroyed. That is, the total mass in the Universe remains constant. Which means, a person, when dead, does not cease to exist but the body mass is distributed to other forms of matter, so that the total mass remains constant. Thus the concept of rebirth as far as body (matter) is concerned is true according to science.

But we have been taught that the body perishes after death while the soul does not perish and how could this be explained? For one thing, this is what we see grossly. That is, we see the inanimate body which means the soul has left the body and the body when burnt, we see the body perishing. Scientifically also, matter has been lost when the body is burnt, only thing is it has been converted to energy and since matter and energy are inter convertible, matter has not actually been lost but converted to energy, whence matter again forms. Thus the concept of rebirth has ratification from three important physical laws namely, the law of conservation of matter, the law of conservation of energy and the famous equation of mass-energy relation of Albert Einstein, namely $E = mc^2$

When an individual dies, the cell also dies. (Death is divided into somatic and molecular death. Somatic death occurs with the cessation of the heart, respiratory and nervous activities. The individual cells are not dead at this juncture which may be delayed, may be up to six hours, usually two hours, after cessation of all vital functions). But the energy trapped in the mitochondria of the cell is still retained inside the cell. That is the reason why it has been said that the body perishes while the soul does not. The evidence to this is from the following:

We use petrol, diesel, kerosene etc for the energy to burn an internal combustion engine, for fuel, etc. These petroleum products are dug from the soil thousands of feet below. They are called fossil fuel and are the energy stored in the mitochondria of cells of animals and plants once lived and fossilized hence. For, fossils are impressions of plants and animals buried in sedimentary rock formations over millions of years. That is, a plant or animal dead millions of years back got entangled in the soil and over the years, soil accumulated over it and finally became part of rocks. The existence of fossils is strong evidence for the Hindu philosophy that only body perishes, the soul does not. Had we not used the fossil fuel, the energy would still be extant, pointing to its eternity.

When, after death, a body is burnt, it burns and crumples to ashes because of the energy trapped in the cells. Were there no energy, the body would not have burnt. That is why a body or a log of wood burns, not stone or a piece of metal.

When an individual dies, energy in the form of heat is given away to the surroundings and thus the body becomes cold. This represents the internal energy (which is partly potential and partly kinetic) which is converted to heat energy. This heat energy is convertible to other forms of energy. The Law of conservation of energy states that energy can neither be created nor be destroyed. Thus the total energy in the Universe remains constant. That is, the energy (soul) of a dead person does not perish, but is converted to another form of energy (another soul). The first Law of Thermo Dynamics is an extrapolation of the Law of conservation of energy and states that heat energy is convertible to other forms of energy.

11

Chapter

ENERGY CHANGES WITH DEATH

When an individual dies, the following changes are noted:

- ✦ The electrical activity of the heart stops and instead of an ECG, a flat line (due to the movement of the graph paper) is recorded.
- ✦ The electrical activity of the brain stops and no EEG waves are recorded.
- ✦ The electro-myograph fails to record any response in the muscle mass.

In short there is no action potential in any cell.

The absence of electrical responses means that the electrical spark which characterized life has ceased to exist. But according to the Law of conservation of energy, the electrical energy cannot simply get lost. It has to be converted to some other form of energy. It cannot be chemical energy as all biochemical activities have come to a standstill. It cannot be mechanical energy as movement is not possible. Then what?

We know that the body immediately after death is still warm and cold sets in a few hours after death. The electrical activity which characterised life got converted to thermal energy which kept the body warm. And when the heat energy dissipates into the environment (moving from a region of higher concentration to a region of lower concentration) the body becomes cold. At this stage, rather at the point of death, the internal energy, which is partly potential and partly kinetic, is also zero.

That this is so is inferred from the following:

Human beings are warm blooded animals i.e. their body temperature does not change with changes in the atmospheric temperature. The normal body temperature in life is 37 degree Celsius and this is so maintained by that part of the brain called hypothalamus. Even slight variations in temperature can produce a host of changes like changes in metabolism, enzymatic action etc. When a man dies the hypothalamus is no longer functional and the temperature regulatory mechanism is not active. Still the body is warm for a few hours and this could only be explained as the conversion of electrical energy into heat energy. After some time the body becomes cold which should not be, because the body should have the same atmospheric temperature. But, because the heat dissipates to the atmosphere, the body becomes cold.

Is energy completely lost with the death of a person? Not at all. Part of the energy dissipates as heat. The rest of the energy is stored in the mitochondria of the cell. When the body is burnt this energy is utilised. If the body is not burnt but is buried, it becomes part of the fossil fuel in the distant future.

12
Chapter

SOUL (ATMA), JEEVATMA, PARAMATMA AND THE ADVAITHA PHILOSOPHY

Stripped to its ridiculous simplicity, *Advaitha* means that there is no duality in soul or in other words there is no difference between what you are and what you see (or sense). Gaudapada is recorded as the earliest proponent but Adi Sankara is reckoned as the staunchest advocate of the *advaitha* philosophy.

The soul or *Atma* within (any) one is the *Jeevatma* or *Antharyami* and the soul outside of self is the *Paramatma*. Various terminologies like Parabrhma and *Aparabrahma*, are used to denote these two entities. We have seen elsewhere that the term *Brahmam* and *AUM* are synonymous and that while AUM represents *Brahmam* as energy, *Brahmam* refers to matter.

Among the Upanishads, the Mandukya Upanishad has the final say where ever the *atma* or soul is considered. The first mantra of the Mandukya Upanishad runs thus:

AUM ithyedaksharam idam sarvam, Thasyopa vyakyanam, bhootam, bhavad,bhavishyad iti, sarvam omkara eva, ya chanyad Trikalatheetam, Thadapi omkara eva.

(All that is seen is AUM. Its most lucid explanation is thus: Past, present or future whatever had existed, exists or will exist in future are all AUM. That which has transgressed the three tenses is also AUM).

The second mantra of the Mandukya Upanishad tells us thus:

> Sarvam hyedad Brahma, ayam atma Brahma,
> Soyamatma chathushpad.

(Whatever has been spoken of about AUM applies to *Brahmam*. This atma is also Brahmam. That *atma* and this *atma* have both four existences).

The four existences of the *atma* are:

1. *Vaiswanaran*
2. *Thaijasan*
3. *Praajnan*
4. *Thureeyan.*

VAISWANARAN

The attributes of the soul as *Vaiswanaran* are described asunder:

> Jagarithashano bahi prajna saptanga ekonavimsathi
> Mukha Sthoolabug vaiswanara pradhama pada

(One who is in the fully awake state, whose *prajna* vests outside of self, having seven members and nineteen faces and enjoys the grosser things in life is *Vaiswanaran* and is the first state of the soul)

A man getting up in the morning, preparing to go to the office, doing office work and all that he does in the wakeful state is in the state of *Vaiswanaran*. In the wakeful state he has two objectives: to keep himself awake and secondly actively participate in the activities of the outside world. This he achieves through his seven members and nineteen faces. The seven members are symbolic representations of the Universe with the *Panchabhoothas* namely Air, Skies, Water, Earth and Fire being represented by the breath, mid body, groin, the feet and the *homa* pyre (the fire in which in which *homas* are performed) respectively and the Heavens and sun by the vertex and eyes. The nineteen faces (*ekonavimsathi mukha* means nineteen faces) with which an individual knows the sentient world refer to the five sense organs or *Jnanendriyas* (eyes, ears, nose, tongue and skin), the five organs of action, *Karmendryas* (the hands, feet, mouth, rectum and genitals) the five breaths (*Pranan, Apanan, Udanan, Vyanan, Samanan*) and the four *anthakaranams* namely instinct, intellect, mind and ego. That is, if he were not to use these *bahyakaranams* and *antha karanams* he would not be in the state of *vaiswanaran*. (If he does not see, smell, hear, feel, or taste, an individual cannot keep awake; nor with his hands and feet really or virtually tied up. With his mind, instinct, intellect or ego laid to rest, he would be a vegetable and if his breath were held he would be dead.)

THIJASAN

Of *Thaijasan*, the description runs thus:

> Swapnasthano antha prajna saptanga
> Ekonavimsathi mukha pravi viktabukh
> Thaijaso dwitheeya pada.

(One who is in the dreamy state, whose *prajna* vests inside of self, with seven members and nineteen faces, who enjoys the finer aspects fabricated by the mind is *Thaijasan* and is the second existence of the soul.)

If *vaiswanaran* refers to the *atma* in the fully awake state, *thaijasan* refers to the *atma* in the dreamy state. Yet it may seem strange that both are credited with the same seven members and nineteen faces. This is because in the dreamy state of *thaijasan*, the mind utilises a portion of the mental impressions that the individual had experienced in the wakeful state. Unlike in the state of *vaiswanaran*, *thaijasan* has no feeders or feelers on which to bank on, to experience the dream it had fabricated. In the dreamy state, the individual can experience any or everything he experienced in the wakeful state: sun or shower, heat or cold, surprise or anger, love or hate. In short though he is not awake, it is as though he were awake. And this is the reason why *thaijasan* is credited with the same seven members and nineteen faces of *vaiswanaran*. With no inputs of the external world, merely depending on the innate talent, this soul enjoys the minute details it has mentally fabricated. Hence it is called *anthaprajna*. Dreams are collages of one's experiences, sensations, imaginations, even extending to fantasies one has over the past built up, and they may or may not be what one had experienced, sensed, heard or imagined and may or may not be real. Since they are not derived from the *panchabhoothas*, they are like impressions in a mirror and hence illusory, though seemingly gross and real as image in a mirror. But once awake and hence out of the dreamy state, their fragile and illusory nature become apparent and dreams tend to be evanescent.

PRAAJNAN

Is the third state of the Atma (Soul) and its attributes are:

Yatra supto na kamchana kamam kamayathe,
na kamchana swapnam pasyathi, tat sushuptam.
Sushuptashana ekibhoota, prajnanakhana
Evanandamayo, hyanandabhuk chethomukha, prajna
sthritiya pada

(Where no desires exist and no dreams are dreamt the state of *Sushuptam* prevails. When in the state of *sushuptam*, when all duality has vanished and singularity prevails, when recoiled from all sensuality and *prajnanam* has solidified, when almost always in bliss and enjoys bliss and with a face that speaks of a mind to return to sensuality, that state is *Prajnan* and is the third state of the *atma*).

Sushupti or deep sleep characterises *Prajnan*. Here ignorance of everything rules. There is neither inner *prajna* nor any outer *prajna* and *prajna* seems solidified. It is an abyss of darkness where nothing, not even self is recognized. Since singularity is not experienced the question of duality does not rise at all. Everything slips into a mass of darkness- hence the term *ekibhootha*. Since nothing could be desired, desires do not exist nor do dreams. Grief and sorrow being not sensed, it is always in bliss. And since on awakening, the presence of a sensation of a sound sleep means that joy and the causative for joy are both present. But *praajnan* has the *chetas* (mind) to return to the dreamy state of *thaijasan* or revert to the state of Praajnan and hence it is called *chethomukhan*.

Physiologists have classified sleep into REM (standing for Rapd Eye Movements) sleep and non REM sleep. For sleep to be complete both these are supposed to be necessary. In the REM phase, there is rapid movement of the eyes and the person dreams. Obviously this is what the state of *thaijasan* stands for. In the non REM phase, there is no movement of the eyeballs and the person is in deep sleep. The REM and non REM states alternate. This is why *Prajnan* (non REM sleep) is called *chethomukhan*- it may slip into the state of *thaijasan (REM Sleep)* or revert to Praajnan.

Delusions, illusions and hallucinations are fabrications of the mind and are present in extremely negligent, transient or evanescent proportions in even normal individuals. For example, we may experience the presence of some one, when actually there is none, our ego may be boosted to the level of a delusion of grandeur, we may experience delusions of persecution, etc. (delusions are experiencing of objects or events which do not exist.) On the contrary an illusion is the mistaking of one object for another, like for example, mistaking a rope for a snake. Hallucinations are the visual or auditory perceptions of the mind when actually these are not there. One may hear the sound of phone bell ringing, or the gate opening when actually none of these has happened. But when these become constant and repeated and violate the sensibility of an individual, he becomes mentally deranged. These rare and other commoner tribulations of the mind are present in the fully awake and dreamy states but never in deep sleep. That may be the reason why a mentally unstable person lacks sleep.

THUREEYAN

Is the fourth state of the *Atma*. Its attributes are:

Na anthaprajnam na bahi prajnam na ubhayatha prajnam
Na prjnana ghanam na prajnam na aprajnam adrisyam
Avyavaharam agrahyam alakshanam achinthyam
Avyapadesam ekatmapratyayasaram prapanchopasamam
santham sivam advaitham chathurtham manyante sa
atma sa vijneyaha

Na anthaprajnam: Not with inner *prajna*. *Antha prajnam* is the soul in the dreamy state and hence *Thaijasan*. The *Atma* is not in the state of *Thaijasan*.

Na bahi prajnam: Not with outer *prajna* i.e. *Vaiswanaran*.

Na ubhayatha prajna: Not with *prajna* inside and outside. The corridor between wakeful and dreamy states is what *ubhayatha prajna* denotes.

Na prajnana ghana: Not with *prajna* solidified. That is, not in the state of *Praajnan*.

Na prajnam: Not one who knows.

Na aprajnam: Not one, who doesn't know.

Adrisyam: One, who is not seen.

Avyavaharam: One with whom no transaction is possible.

Agrahyam: One, who could not be understood.

Alakshanam: One with no signs.

Achinthyam: One, who could not be thought of.

Avyapadesam: Not known by a name.

Ekatmaprathyayasaram: Known only because there is but one *atma*. If you ask whether there is *atma* in this body the answer is yes because there is *atma* in you, *atma* in me, *atma* in everything in the universe and that is one and the same *atma* and hence there is *atma* in this body also.)

Prapanchopasamam: one in whom the changes in nature evoke no response.

Santham: serene.

Sivam: Pure.

Advaitham: with no alternate.

Chathurtham: fourth.

Manyanthe: is thought of.

Sa: He

Atma: *atma*

Sa: he

Vijneya: to be known

One who is not with inner *prajna* (*Thaijasan*), outer *prajna* (*Vaiswanaran*), nor with inner and outer *prajna* (the corridor between *Thaijasan* and *Viswanaran*), *Prajna* solidified (*Praajnan*), not with *prajna*, not without *prajna*, one who cannot be seen, interacted or understood, one with no sign, one who cannot be imagined or called by a name, one whose existence is known only because the same *atma* is present in every object in the universe, one who is unresponsive to the moods of nature, one who is serene, pure and without an alternate is the fourth existence of the soul. That is the soul, the one to be known.

I see a lady. (Is it a she? It could as well be a pot bellied man) She has a bulging belly. I am not sure what the bulge is due to. Is there a life inside? I am not sure (*agrahyam*). I cannot see what is behind the bulge (*adrisyam*). I cannot transact with whatever is inside (*avyavaharam*). I cannot think what is inside (*achinthyam*- it may be a foetus but not necessarily so. There are other conditions like fat, fluid, faeces, flatus etc which can cause a similar appearance or a condition called pseudocyesis where a lady, for all appearances is pregnant, but is not actually pregnant). There are no signs pointing to what it could be (*alakshanam*). I cannot call it by a name even (*avyapadesam*- if it were a boy, I could have called him he, if a girl, she but here it is impossible). It shows no sign of *prajna* outside (*bahiprajna*) or *prajna* inside (*anthaprajna*). One cannot say whether prajna has solidified (*Praajnan*) or whether it is in the corridor between *anthaprajna* and *bahiprajna- ubhayadoprajna*. It does not seem affected by the moods of nature (*prapanchopasamam*). The only way I could presume there is *atma* in it is by assuming that since *atma* is present in all and that *atma* is the same in all beings in the universe, there is bound to be the same *atma* inside also (*ekatma pratyayasaram*). It is serene and shows no activity (*santham*). It is pure (*sivam*)- there is nothing to taint it. And it is without alternate (*advaitham*). It is this *atma* (sa atma), the one which has to be recognized (sa vijneya) as the fourth (chathurtham) existence of the soul. Obviously the foetus inside the mother's womb fulfils all the criteria laid out for *thureeyan*.

A hen is brooding over eggs. By appearance, you cannot distinguish it from the egg you are about to swallow. Is there a life pulsating inside? You are not sure.

You plough land and sow seeds. You know nothing of what happens in the sub soil. The seeds may have germinated or it might not have. Until the growing seedlings break open the soil and start sprouting, you cannot say that life ever existed in the sub soil.

In short, the *in camera* life when germination has started but life has not breathed the outside air, whether in a germinating seed or in a fertilized egg developing into an embryo or a foetus in its mother's womb, life languishing inside meets all the criteria prescribed for *thureeyan*. Our teachers taught *thureeyan* as a state of extreme bliss and the one state every *atma* cherishes to attain, probably because they did not attribute *thureeyan* to be the incognito, incommunicado life of a foetus, but as the stage next to God realisation or supreme bliss. This is because they considered only the normal states of the *atma* and ignored the special situation, the not repeated state of the *atma* which happens only once in the entire life of the *atma* or the individual and that is the life *in utero*. It is pertinent to note that nowhere is it mentioned that *thureeyan* is a state of the *atma* in extreme bliss.

Let us revert to *thureeyan* and view it from another angle. From the description of the state of *thureeyan*, it is clear that this existence of the *atma* is one where there is no semblance of life- so called hanging to life by a thread. The only way it could be presumed to be present is by what is called *ekatmapratyaya saram*. That is, this *atma* is there because there is *atma* in you, there is *atma* in me, there is *atma* in every object in the universe and since this is one and the same *atma* the *atma* in *thureeyan* is also the same *atma*. On a perusal of the mantra, it is obvious that it mentions only about the negative aspects of life. Nowhere is mentioned that it is a state of bliss. In the state of Vaiswanaran the *atma* enjoys the sentient world from inputs from the sense organs. In the dreamy state or *thijasan*, the mind fabricates and enjoys what it has witnessed in dream. In *sushupti* (deep sleep) i.e. the state of *Praajnan*, the *atma* is described as *anandamaya* (primarily in bliss) and *anandabuk* (one who enjoys bliss) while in the state of *thureeyan*, bliss is a thing never mentioned. Leave alone bliss, none of the life characteristics - joy, sorrow, anger, hunger, thirst, lust, warmth, cold- is the attribute of *thureeyan*; statistically speaking, 99.99% dead. In other words, the state of *thureeyan* is a state of the *atma* wedged in between the ultimate (death) and the penultimate (*sushupti*) or between *sushupthi* and *jagrath* (*vaiswanaran*). (The existence of the soul or *atma* could be called a constant "march to death." From the moment life appears in a body, it is relentlessly marching to death. From a daily basis it could be considered as the four states of the *atma* and from a life time basis the four stages like boyhood, adolescence, youth and old age). And from full vivacity in the fully awake state, life languishes in the dreamy state and near total inactivity in the *sushupti* state. And the next state is death or total inactivity or reversion to the original state of activity or *viswanaran*. So *thureeyan* is not a normal state of the *atma*, but one that occurs very rarely namely once when a life is forming or when life is just leaving the body. In other words **thureeyan is**

the unmanifested state of the atma till life makes itself manifest or till it just leaves the body.

Of *thureeyan,* it has been said that it is with *prajna* and without *prajna.* This may seem unlikely as how anyone could be with and without *prajna* at the same time. We have seen elsewhere that *Prajnanam* is *Brahmam* and *prajna* is present in all objects, living or dead, small or big. Hence the statement that *thureeyan* is with *prajna* holds good. On the contrary, it has been said that *thureeyan* is without *bahi prajna* or *prajna* outside, without *antha prajna* or *prajna* inside and without *ubayatha prajna* or *prajna* in the gray zone between *antha prajna* and *bahiprajna* which means for all appearances it can be presumed that there is no *prajna* at all.

There is expressed in this mantra a couple of words: *Sa atma, Sa vijneya* meaning he is the *atma,* he is the one to be known. What it implies is that this is a state of the *atma* which has to be recognized as such. If you recognize it as an *atma* which has life in it, you could still bring it back to normal life by appropriate means. On the contrary, if you do not recognize it as state of the *atma,* you might consider it dead.

What does all this amount to? An *atma* (person) who is not active, dreamy, or sleepy, whose existence cannot be visualized, imagined or inferred, who is neither conscious nor unconscious, who responds to none of the natural stimuli, like heat cold etc., who cannot be called by a name even (a living man could be called Mr. So and so and a dead man as the late Mr. So and so, but here neither is possible), serene because it cannot become agitated even if it so desires, pure because nothing could possibly taint it, known only by the beautiful word *ekatmapratyaya saram.*

Well, *thureeyan* is next only to death or just a throw away from life. We have seen how this satisfies in pregnancy. Let us now consider the other condition where it is inches from death. The only difference between death and *thureeyan* is that life could still be brought back while in death it is not possible. Medical experts call this (state of the *atma*) as suspended animation. Here the heart and lungs might have stopped functioning and the muscles become stiff but the individual could be brought back to life by electric shock, cardiac massage etc.

I invite you to three instances: You are talking to someone and while happily talking to you the man stumbles and falls. In panic, you ask for water to be fetched and sprinkle it on his face, thinking it as a fainting episode. You lay him on a couch and in the meantime people have closed in. Someone suggests a doctor be called. By the time the doctor comes, it is thirty five minutes. He looks at the non respiring body, finds no pulse, the blood pressure is un-recordable, no heart sounds could be heard and the pupils are widely dilated and the cornea lustreless. He pronounces the person dead due to cardiac arrest.

In the second instance, you are travelling in a railway coach. The man sitting in front of you slowly turns on his side. At first you think that the man is going to sleep, but soon you realize that the man is almost absolutely inert and his position is maintained without fall only because the man next to him had been inadvertently supporting him. On an impulse, you, though not a medical man but trained in cardiopulmonary resuscitation (CPR), feel for his pulse, find none and realize that the man has gone into cardiac arrest. You lay him on the floor, face up and start cardio pulmonary resuscitation. After, may be, fifteen minutes, the man wakes up as though from a sleep and moves about as if nothing has happened.

Cardiac arrest can occur in hospital situations as well. In the third setting, you are a doctor in the Intensive care unit. A patient who has been admitted an hour ago is under treatment for heart attack. Just when you are doing all the required treatment, the patient suddenly goes into cardiac arrest. The ECG shows a straight line. The cardiologist springs into action and with the defibrillator applies 240 v current over the chest. And the patient sits up coughing (not necessarily).

As a doctor, I had witnessed all the situations mentioned. While doctors use the terminology cardiac arrest to denote the sudden cessation of the activity of the heart and the term **suspended animation** to describe the condition simulating death thereafter, the Upanishads use the term *thureeeyan* to describe this situation. It is important to recognize the existence of such an entity, for precious life could be saved if correct treatment is given by anybody at the proper time (not that this is always possible). That is why the Mandukya Upanishad uses the term *sa atma, sa vijneya* meaning he is the *atma*, he is the one to be known while describing the term *thureeyan*.

Suspended animation is not confined to cardiac arrest but is also known in cases of shock, anaesthesia, yoga, cholera, trance, hysteria, drowning, sun stroke, and sometimes in still born infants and has been a tool with cardio-thoracic surgeons as an artificially induced state during cardiac surgeries to sustain life during surgery.

Way back in 1982, I was working as the Medical Officer, Government Rural Dispensary, Vadavannur when one day a lady was brought to me, walking, with the complaint of having passed loose stools twice. Finding it as a case of simple diarrhoea with all the vital signs intact, I prescribed some anti-diarrhoeal to her and sent her home. In less than a couple of hours, she was brought back to me carried by four people with no pulse, no recordable BP, no respiration, totally dehydrated and with no viable parameters. I had her removed to the hospital and I started a drip in each of her limbs running full throttle. And after about ten bottles had gone in about two hours, did she open her eyes and I get a palpable pulse. And where her excursions were during this time? Obviously she was in the corridor between life and death. (Not that she was in suspended animation for about two hours and came back to life with the infusion-No. She could have gone into suspended animation any time after her heart stopped pumping and reverted to normal any time after start of the infusion.) A stool examination report was to come later as positive for cholera. She walked back to life after a couple of days.

Having spoken of the four states of the soul or *atma*, a comparison is made as to how it equates with the Omnipotent, Omnipresent, Omniscient power on the Universe or *Paramatma* or *Parabrhma*, for this is the crux of the *advaita* philosophy. The eighth mantra of the Mandukya Upanishad tells thus. In the ninth mantra, how the first syllable A compares with the first existence of the soul is described:

Jagaritha sthano vaiswanarokara pradama matra apter-
Adimathvad va apnoti ha Y sarvan kamanadischa bhavati
ya evam veda

(By virtue of being all pervasive or being primordial, *vaiswanaran* whose status is wakefulness equates with the first syllable A in AUM. One who recognizes as such will have all his desires fulfilled and he becomes foremost among the elite).

The first existence of the soul is soul in the wakeful state or *Vaiswanaran*. The first syllable in AUM is A. That is relative to U or M, A is the syllable first uttered. Likewise compared to *thaijasan* or *prajnan, vaiswanaran* occupies the position number one. That is one similarity. *Vaiswanaran* in the virad form expands into the whole universe, just like A as the basis of all sound sans which, no language, no communication is possible the world over. (The syllable A in AUM is produced on opening the mouth and no word could be uttered without opening the mouth). In the same way, we get to know about the universe in the wakeful state. One who knows as such would have all his dreams fulfilled

One may wonder as to how the knowledge that the soul in the wakeful state or the syllable A in AUM could fulfil all the desires or make one become the foremost among the elite. Chant the syllable A, a million times or repeat that you know *Viswanaran* as the all pervasive and primordial equivalent to A, nothing happens. So where is the catch?

Soul in the wakeful state is the one which keeps track of worldly affairs. One knows the happenings in the world only because one is awake. In the dreamy state of *thaijasan* or deep sleep of *Praajnan,* one cannot do any work or know of a thing which happens around him or anywhere in the world. So one who knows that *Viswanaran* or the wakeful state is the one which earns him his bread or wins him wars, will utilise his wakeful state to full advantage and win laurels. It is in the wakeful state that man moves into action and does all things. Great scientists were born because they worked in their wakeful hours. Great empires, great civilizations, great projects were all the result of soul in the wakeful state-never when the soul was dreaming, never when the soul was in deep slumber.

Likewise is the syllable A in AUM. The syllable A, it has been said, is the basis of all syllables, languages, communication. One who realizes this and utilizes this knowledge becomes foremost among the elite. Macaulay as an orator, Shakespere as a writer, Birbal as a jester or Thenali Raman as a courtier all find their names writ large in the annals of history because they realised this and put this knowledge to their advantage. So anyone who opens his mouth and puts practical wisdom in his spoken words carries with him the masses. One who remains incommunicado achieves nothing. This is the message conveyed in this mantra.

Swapna sthanas thijasa ukaro dwitheeya
Matra utkareshad ubhayathvad vauthkarsathi
Ha y jnana sandhathim samanascha bhavathi
Nya sya brahmavith kule bhavathi ya evam veda

(The second syllable in AUM, U equates with the second existence of the soul namely *Thaijasan* which has its status in the dreamy state. Both have in common pre eminence and duality i.e. the proclivity to turn to either side, as their common attributes. One who knows this attains prosperity and becomes wiser and respectable. His lineage would not have anyone sans Brahmajnanam).

The soul in the dreamy state of *thaijasan* has two attributes: the ability to revert to Praajnan on one side or as *Thaijasan* on the other. A person attains heights only if he has dreams. When one dreams of becoming a King, it remains as a motive for him to attain great heights. It is thus the driving force which propels a person to activity. "One has occasionally to gaze at the stars even though one may not reach them" Nehru said. One who never gazes at the stars may not have the inclination to reach the stars. Had man not gazed at the moon, he might not have landed on the moon. And if he had thought the Mars too far away, he might not have tried even to dream landing on the Mars. In other words, just as *Praajnan (somnolence) represents Srishti, thaijasan* is responsible for the idea behind doing things. Sans dreams, actions might not have followed.

The second attribute of *thaijasan* is said to be its duality i.e. it can turn to *Praajnan* (somnolence) or slip back into Thaijasan. What is meant here is that a person who had dreamt of a thing could either execute his dreams or sleep over what he had dreamt. Not all dreams are followed by action. Some of the dreams of some of the persons find fruition while many a dream may remain a dream slipping into oblivion or somnolence (*Praajnan*). Thus it is the poised state showing neither the hyper activity of *Vaiswanaran* nor the deadly inactivity of *Prajnan*. This is what the term 'ubhayathavad va' means. A person with a vision, a dream, or an innovative idea becomes the object of respect of all.

Sushupta sthana prajno makara striteeya matra
Mithera peetherva minoti ha va
Idam sarvama peethischa bhavati ya evam veda

(The third syllable in AUM, M vests its place in somnolence (deep sleep-*sushupti*). Their common virtues are measure and oneness. One who understands as such, measures the whole world i.e. understands the whole world and identifies with the *atma* that is the cause of the Universe). Now what does this mean? Let us first recapitulate the attributes of the soul in the state of *Praajnan*. That state where there are no wants, where there are no dreams (*sushuptam*), where no duality exists, where the *prajna* is solidified, where all sensations are withdrawn, where one is in bliss and enjoys bliss, where one has the face that beckons return to sensuality, that state is *Praajnan*.

A man in deep sleep-*sushupti*- has no wants and there are no dreams either (Dreams occur only in the state of *thaijasan*). Here the conscience does not work and darkness solidifies both inside and outside. And since self itself is not recognized, nothing else is recognized. In other words, he is insensitive to all sensations. Yet, in spite of lack of sensations, he enjoys his sleep as otherwise people wouldn't have said: "Had a good sleep; didn't know a thing." Which means, though he did not know anything in sleep, he knew that he enjoyed the sleep. That means the sensation of pleasure was there. That is why it is said that *Praajnan* has the face that shows his mind's willingness to return to sensuality. Since nothing, not even self is recognized there is no duality but everything merges into one solid mass of nought.

How does the soul as *Praajnan* equate with the syllable M in AUM? M in AUM stands for *srishti* or creation. A seed becomes a tree and we call it creation. For a seed to grow into a tree it lies dormant for a period of time i.e. the seed is in a state as *Praajnan* or *sushupti* or deep sleep. The seed cannot lie dormant for any length of time. In other words its period of dormancy is fixed and pre determined. That is why it is said that one of the attributes of M or *srishti* is measure. A sperm or an ovum remains dormant before it is released and the period of dormancy of the sperm or ovum is fixed and these may become non viable over a period of time, if the ovum is not fertilized by the sperm. Similarly the next attribute, namely, oneness, of both Prajnan and the syllable M or srishti denotes the fusion of anthaprajna of thaijasan and bahiprajna of vaiswanaran into one of prajnanaghana in praajnan and fusion of a male gamete(sperm) with a female gamete (ovum) into one solid mass of cells or zygote which develops into a baby.

Thureeyan is the fourth state of the *atma* and equates with the fourth syllable in AUM. The fourth syllable in AUM is described as *amatra*. But here the explanations given by our seers are rather difficult to digest. Their interpretation is that just as three quarters unite and complete a whole rupee, so the amalgamation of *Viswanaran, Thaijasan* and *Praajnan* results in a unified one called *thureeyan*. This explanation results from the fact that they were left only with three syllables for AUM and four existences for the *atma* and hence equating became difficult. This explanation is flawed from many angles and hence the interpretation is untenable. For one thing, three quarters do not make a whole rupee but four quarters do. Secondly, if the amalgamation of *Viswanaran, Thaijasan* and *Prajnan* were to become *Thureeyan*, then the whole set of qualities which characterized *thureeyan* would become void. Also the term *amatra* used to qualify the syllable equivalent to *thureeyan* would become void as A+U+M would amount to AUM and not to *amatra*. Fourthly, the second mantra of the Mandukya Upanishad says that the *atma* has four parts or existences which are distinct and hence *thureeyan* is a distinct entity and not the amalgamated form of the other three. In view of the above, a re-look at AUM and *thureeyan*, keeping in mind what has been already said of both is worth the while.

When we pronounce the word AUM, it sounds like a simple OM. But putting life into it, we find that the sound originates in our belly. As the sound travels up, it picks up resonance as the word AUM is pronounced, trailing into an after-resonance before ending in total silence. While writing, we can only write AUM and cannot represent the resonance or after-resonance. That is, this after resonance is very much a part of AUM without being seen (*adrisyam*), known by outward descriptions (*Na bahi prajnam*), understood (*agrahyam*), not thought of (*achinthyam*), with no qualities (*alakshanam*), not known by a name (*avyapadesam*). And since it cannot be called by a syllable even, (*avyapadesam*), it is called *amatra* (Non syllable). Thus this *amatra* or after-resonance has all the attributes of *thureeyan* and like *thureeyan* is known only by *ekatmapratyayasaram*. That is, this after-resonance is known only because of the resonance in A, the resonance in U and the resonance in M, sans which this after-resonance has no existence. Trying to utter the after-resonance without uttering the resonating A, U and M will be impossible. So the existence of the after-resonance is known only because of the resonance in

A,U, and M. Carried further, we find that this resonance and after-resonance are the same wherever resonance is created, whatever be the situation

Having spoken about *thureeyan*, the question now is what happens to *thureeyan*. We have seen that the states of the *atma* are *Vaiswanaran, thaijasan, Prajnan* and *thureeyan*, the last named as a distinct entity, not always present, but a state of the *atma* none the less. So, after *thureeyan*, it is either the *atma* returning as *Vaiswanaran* or death.

Let us examine the whole concept of the *atma* or soul in a scientific way. We know the body is composed of a framework we call the body and the energy (soul) which propels it into activity just as in a car with a body and an engine. In other words it is the soul (*atma*) which propels the body and in its absence the individual is dead. Hence soul may be defined as that which gives momentum to the body. Equated it means energy. Since energy is required for doing all work, a body bereft of energy may be considered inanimate or dead. Even when the body is apparently inactive, energy is utilised for maintaining the basic functions of the body namely respiration, circulation etc. (In the state of *praajnan*, the body is inactive and the soul is inactive, but the individual is alive).

This concept is well documented by Physicists. They teach us that energy of a body is its ability to do work. Energy is of different types like mechanical, electrical, chemical, thermal, sound, light, nuclear etc. Living organisms have mechanical energy and thermal energy (which is due to the cell metabolism), electrical energy etc. Man gets energy for doing work and sustaining life from the food he eats. The food we eat contains carbohydrates, fats and proteins. By the action of enzymes, the carbohydrates are broken down into glucose which is the easily assimilated form and this glucose is carried by circulation to the remotest cells in the body and in the cell, by the action of many enzymes is converted into pyruvic acid, lactic acid, citric acid etc. During this process energy is liberated in the form of ATP (adenosine tri phosphate) and water and the energy thus liberated is stored in the mitochondria of the cell. This ATP provides energy for the cellular activity and in turn the activity of the individual.

The food we eat also contains proteins which are broken down by the enzymes into amino acids (which are the building blocks and along with fats contribute to the cell wall structure),which are necessary for production of hormones, enzymes etc. Fats in the food are converted to tri-glycerides, cholesterol etc and are taken up for various body requirements (like vitamin D absorption, cell wall synthesis, etc) and the excess fat is deposited as fat depots in the adipose tissue (predominantly in the abdomen where it displays as pot belly). In exigencies this fat is utilized and converted to glucose and serves as the source of energy and answers how life is maintained in the absence of food even up to four weeks.

We often speak of the spark of life which indeed it is. It is an electrical spark which propels the body into action. Every cell in the body shows electrical activity. If an electrician connects two terminals to a multi meter ('multi' they call it), it shows a deflection of the needle if the circuit is intact. When two electrodes are placed over the cell surface, no electrical activity is observed (for observing electrical activity in a cell, the deflections are magnified by a magnifier and viewed through a Cathode-Ray-Oscilloscope.) But when one of the electrodes is inserted into the cell, a deflection of the needle occurs, pointing to a potential difference between the interior and the exterior of the cell. (This potential difference is called resting membrane potential). The resting membrane potential is usually negative (inside cell is negative and outside positive). When an electrical current is passed through the cell, reversal of the resting state occurs, inside becomes positive and outside negative. This is called a depolarized state. Status quo is maintained after some time, the interior becomes negative and outside positive and this state is called a re-polarized state. Together (depolarisation-repolarisation) they constitute what is called an action potential.

The play of action potential is evident in day to day life. The ECG (electro-cardio-graph) recording the electrical activity of the heart, EEG (electro encephalography) recording the electrical activity of the brain are all too well known. (Other recordings include electro myography, electro retinography, electro nystagmography etc). Only, these are mass responses of groups of cells, not single cells.

Who or what provides the electrical impulse for activity? In the case of the heart muscle, a tiny mass of modified cardiac muscle called the sino-atrial node (SA node) situated in the right atrium provides the impulse. This tissue is called the pace maker of the heart. In the case of muscles, the electrical impulse is provided by the brain.

How is an electrical impulse or action potential generated? A cell has a cell membrane which holds all the constituents of the cell (called cell organelles) together in its fold. Two contiguous cells are separated by a small space which contains a fluid called extracellular fluid. The outside of the cell is positive and the inside negative. This negativity inside is maintained by a sodium-potassium pump which moves two sodium ions into the cell and three potassium ions outside of the cell. The energy for this is provided by ATP (derived from the glucose in the food we eat). Since more positive ions are pumped out of the cell, the inside of the cell is negative.

Thus ATP provides the energy for activating the sodium-potassium pump, which creates an ionic imbalance and this in turn is responsible for the depolarisation followed by repolarisation or an action potential and this action potential is the basis of nervous, muscular, cardiac etc. activity. Thus the basis of life is an electrical charge, and electrical charge has a positive component, a negative component and a neutral component.

The second factor leading to an electrical negativity in the cell is what is called the selective permeability of the cell membrane. Large negatively charged molecules like proteins, phosphate, sulphate etc are retained inside the cell and do not move across the cell membrane. But potassium, sodium, chloride ions move across the cell membrane based on certain principles. This creates the negativity inside the cell and the sequence of electrical activities which follow.

Thus the electrical spark which is the basis of all life with a positive charge, a negative charge and electrical neutrality is called *Jeevatma* (AUM) in Upanishad parlance while the atomic structure which is the basis of all matter with a positive charge, negative charge and neutrality is called *Brahmam*. And the Mandukya Upanishad tells in no uncertain terms that the *Jeevatma* and *Paramatma* are one and the same or AUM is Brahmam. This is the advaita philosophy. In scientific parlance, any object in the Universe, living or non living, atom small or mountain big has two constituents, namely, matter and energy. And these are guided by two universal laws, namely the Law of conservation of mass and the law of conservation of energy which prove what the Upanishads teach us.

13
Chapter

THE UNIVERSAL TRUTH AND THE UNIVERSAL LAWS

The study of AUM teaches us one Universal truth: Any object in the Universe, living or dead, however big or however small, has two constituents, namely, AUM and Brahmam and both are the same. These, in other words, are called the Jeevatma and the Paramatma respectively. That both these are the same form the crux of the Advaita philosophy. Scientists call them energy and matter respectively. In 1808, Dalton, the Swedish Chemist, enunciated the atomic theory, the main postulates of which are:

1. Matter is composed of very small and indivisible particles called atoms.(Atom, in Greek, means that which cannot be divided).

2. Each element has atoms of the same size, shape and mass, which differ with different elements.

3. Atoms are the smallest units taking part in chemical reactions.

4. Atoms combine in simple whole number ratio to form molecules.

5. Atoms are indestructible with physical or chemical change.

The first postulate of Dalton has been beautifully illustrated in the Mahavakya *That Tvm ASi*:

Sa ya yeshonam ithatatmam idam sarvam
That satym sa atma that tvm asi Svetaketo iti

(The infinitesimally minute aspect or core is the *atma* of the whole Universe. That alone is the truth and the *Atma* of all, O! Svetaketo, That Thou Art).

It has already been said that the whole Universe is AUM or Brahmam, Brahmam and AUM are matter and energy and hence whatever has been said of matter applies to Brahmam.

Based on Dalton's postulates, the Law of conservation of matter was propounded which states that matter can neither be created nor be destroyed (but is converted from one form to another). Therefore the total matter in the universe remains constant.

Michael Faraday found that when electricity was passed through solutions, atoms acquired charges. But atoms as such are electrically neutral. An atom has a central nucleus composed of positively charged particles or protons and electrically neutral particles called neutrons. Electrically negative particles called electrons, whose number equal the number of protons, move in fixed orbits round the nucleus and since the positive and negative charges are equal, atoms are electrically neutral. In solution or when electricity is passed through it, an atom loses or gains electrons. The atoms which gain an electron become negatively charged and move toward the anode while atoms which lose electrons become positively charged and move toward the cathode. The atoms which have acquired charge are called ions. Thus Faraday's experiments prove that in solution also atoms (or AUM) exist.

We have seen elsewhere that soul (a*tma*) is an electrical spark which kindles life and an electrical impulse also has a positive phase, a negative phase and electrical neutrality. And electricity is one form of energy. It has been mentioned at the start that AUM is a sonic form of Brahmam. So whether Brahmam exists as sound, electricity or any other form of energy like internal energy, mechanical, radiant, chemical, electromagnetic etc. one form of it could be converted to the other. This leads us to the second universal law namely Law of conservation of energy which states that whenever energy is converted from one form to one or more of the other forms, there is no loss or gain of energy. In other words, energy can neither be created nor be destroyed.

The most significant of all scientific principles is probably the mass-energy relation of Albert Einstein which states that a mass m is equivalent to an amount of energy E given by the relation

$E = mc^2$

Where c is the velocity of light in vacuum. Thus mass and energy are equivalent. That is, mass can be converted into energy and vice versa. (This is what happens when cooking gas is generated from wastes-mass is converted to energy. During photosynthesis, plants absorb carbon dioxide from the atmosphere and in presence of sunlight and water convert it into glucose which is utilised by the plant as the source of energy. Here, light energy is getting converted to chemical energy.) This in essence is the *advaita* philosophy which states that *jeevatma* and *paramatma* are one and the same. It also proves what has often been said: that after death of a person, the body perishes while the soul is immortal. True, after death the body may be burnt or decomposed, but the energy liberated lives on with no chance to get destroyed, only to be transformed.

In conclusion it maybe said that Scientists of the last two centuries 'invented' what our sages have 'discovered' ages before.